Changing Course
Real-Life Stories from Gig Harbor

This book was written for the express purpose of conveying the love and mercy of Jesus Christ. The statements in this book are substantially true; however, names and minor details have been changed to protect people and situations from accusation or incrimination.

Published in Beaverton, Oregon, by Good Catch Publishing.
www.goodcatchpublishing.com
V1.1

Printed in the United States of America

Table of Contents

Dedication

This book is dedicated to all those seeking to change the course of their story.

Acknowledgements

I would like to thank Tyson Lash for the hard work he put into this book to make it a reality. I'm also grateful to Amy Lash for the vision she had from the beginning and the effort she put into making this book come to life. And to the people of Harbor Life, thank you for your boldness and vulnerability in letting us "see" you in this compilation of real-life stories.

This book would not have been published without the amazing efforts of our Project Manager, Jeannette Scott. Her untiring resolve pushed this project forward and turned it into a stunning victory. Thank you for your great fortitude and diligence. Deep thanks to our Editor in Chief, Michelle Cuthrell, and Executive Editor, Nicole Phinney Lowell, for all the amazing work they do. I would also like to thank our invaluable Proofreader, Melody Davis, for all the focus and energy she has put into perfecting our words.

Lastly, I want to extend our gratitude to the creative and very talented Ann Clayton, who designed the beautiful cover for *Changing Course: Real-Life Stories from Gig Harbor.*

Daren Lindley
President and CEO
Good Catch Publishing

The book you are about to read
is a compilation of authentic life stories.
The facts are true, and the events are real.
These storytellers have dealt with crisis, tragedy, abuse
and neglect and have shared their most private moments,
mess-ups and hang-ups in order for others to learn and
grow from them. In order to protect the identities of those
involved in their pasts, the names and details of some
storytellers have been withheld or changed.

Introduction

Story is the language of the heart. We understand it. We are drawn to it. *We live it.* This is why we are moved by stories that inspire change and promise redemption. This is why we root for the underdog and get angry at injustice. This is why we feel robbed when the story doesn't end the way we want it to. Something deep inside of us was created to connect with story.

What about your story? Is there disconnect in your story? What do you do when you don't like how it's being written? When your story seems to be running out of control? When your search isn't producing the results you are looking for? When bad news catches you by surprise? Can you escape the shadow of your past? Will the darkness of depression ever leave? Is change even possible?

The course of your life *can* change. You *can* turn over a new leaf. It is possible to become a new person. The very inspiration you need to write a new chapter may be written on the pages of this book. It was written with you in mind.

Expect inspiration, hope and transformation! As you walk with each real person from our very own city through the pages of this book, you will not only find riveting accounts of their hardships, you will learn the secrets that changed the course of their life stories. These people are no longer living in the shadows of yesterday. They are no longer discontent and disconnected. They are thriving with a sense of mission and purpose TODAY. May these stories inspire you to experience the same.

Leaving Vietnam

The Story of Ray Tabares

Written by Marty Minchin

The news from President Lyndon B. Johnson came as a surprise. Married men without children were no longer exempt from the Vietnam War draft — unless they married by August 26, 1965.

That gave me about six hours to find a wife.

My best candidate was Linda, who I picked up for a date that night in my 1961 Ford Galaxy. She was a cute girl, but we'd only been seeing each other about six weeks. We were only teenagers, way too young to have talked about marriage on our Saturday night dates.

"How about getting married?" There really wasn't a good way to approach the matter. "Tonight. We can drive straight to Coeur d'Alene."

Linda stammered out her answer. "Ray, you know I can't do that. I want to go to college."

Linda wasn't the kind of girl to fall for a quickie marriage. She had other plans for her life, and even if we did get married, what kind of future could I offer her as a farm wife?

I didn't take her turndown personally. Without a marriage certificate, all I could do was wait for my brown envelope from the U.S. government.

Changing Course

Life on my dad's farm in Yakima, Washington, was all I had ever known. When I wasn't in school, I was working, often past dark. We had 890 acres of land near a sugar beet factory, and the root vegetable was our primary crop. When the plant shut down, we diversified to cantaloupes, tomatoes and watermelons. My dad owned the farm with his brother, and my brother, Richard, and I were their main helpers.

We took Saturdays off and went to church on Sundays. I knew that if I ever wanted to get married and have children, I'd have to leave the farm. Any woman I married and any children I had would need me to provide and be around. Farm life required backbreaking work and paid low wages.

Outside our world in the Yakima Valley, the Vietnam War raged. My teenage friends and I were a prime target for the draft.

Some of them jumped the Canadian border to dodge it. When I graduated from Wapato High School in 1964, I didn't feel good about following their lead, even though I knew my name would come up eventually.

One Saturday morning right after graduation, my cousin Jack, our friend John and I drove 160 miles to Seattle to take the entrance test for the U.S. Air Force. If I was called up in the draft, I'd go straight into the U.S. Army, and I didn't want to be a "ground pounder." This was a pre-emptive move.

We all passed the test, and my background working on farm machinery qualified me as an airplane mechanic.

Jack and John joined right up, but I had to talk to my father first.

Our conversation didn't go well. I told him I didn't want to be a farmer. He didn't understand why I had decided to go into the military, and he was hurt that I had taken the test. Richard had left home, and if I went, too, Dad would have to hire men to take our place.

Dad stopped talking to me for a while. Mom, always the peacemaker, got tired of the silence.

"Just go out and talk to him," she urged, nodding toward the field. My dad was a faint dot in the wide expanse of sugar beets.

I strode through the crops, determined to close the divide growing between us.

"Dad, I'll stay." That got his attention. "I'll help you bring in the crop for one more year. But if the Air Force calls me up, I'll have to leave."

He stopped working and clapped me on the back. We forged a truce, and I think he understood that he couldn't force me to stay.

"Ray!" my mom called, running across the field where my dad and I were harvesting sugar beets on an October afternoon two months after I had proposed to Linda.

Even at a distance, I could see the brown paper waving in my mom's hand. I had instructed her not to open any official-looking envelopes, but she clearly hadn't listened.

Changing Course

The Vietnam War was still young, and anti-war sentiment had yet to build. I was raised in a Catholic church, and fighting and killing people went against everything I believed. On the farm, we only killed the animals we would eat. I had been in only two or three fights in my life. I had never been away from home.

The outside of the envelope read, "Greetings."

The words inside would change my life:

You are hereby ordered for induction into the Armed Forces of the United States …

I had one week to report to U.S. Army facilities, which I had no intention of doing. I went straight to my Air Force recruiter, and two days later, I was a serviceman. It was either this or stick it out at the farm, and I wanted something better out of life, even if that meant going to war.

In my youth, I had tried to find meaning in life through church. My family attended faithfully throughout my childhood, and I served as an usher. After I got my driver's license, I often chauffeured our priest around to labor camps where he would meet with people and do ministry. I was a faithful member of Knights of Columbus — a Catholic fraternal society that helped people in need — and I sponsored many young men who wanted to join.

But in the early 1960s, the news reports of astronomical deaths in Vietnam made me wonder whether God was really on my side. The draft was a question of when, not if, for me, and I needed a sign from God that he was behind me and that everything would be okay. It never came. By October 1965, I had pretty much stopped going to church.

Why did you decide this is what you had in store for me? I asked God, reading my draft notice over and over. I wondered what would happen to me in Vietnam. Would I die? Would I come home a wacko?

As far as I was concerned, I didn't have much to talk to God about. I'm not sure if I even believed anymore that he existed.

The plane trip from Seattle to Texas took me into an entirely new world. I had just turned 20, and I had never been far from Yakima, much less on an airplane. I landed at Dyess Air Force Base in Abilene, Texas, where I would attend aircraft mechanic school.

After more schooling, I was sent to New Jersey for temporary duty, where I was assigned to a crew and a plane. We waited for our call to Vietnam.

When the staff sergeant summoned us to a big meeting in 1967, my heart raced with anxiety. This was the day. *Oh, God, what did I do to deserve this?*

We were allowed two weeks of vacation before flying west into our uncertain future. I went home to Washington, where my parents had moved to Seattle after losing the farm. My dad just couldn't make it work anymore.

The flight to Vietnam seemed never-ending. We stopped in Guam and Hawaii to refuel before landing in the Philippines. It was winter when I left the United States, and days later, I stepped out into nearly 100-degree weather. The treeless, barren desert was a far cry from the green lushness of Washington State. I couldn't understand the language of the locals. Everything was different.

After six weeks in the Philippines, we finally were sent to Vietnam and stationed near the South China Sea. Monsoon season was at its height, and I sweated so much from the humidity that most days I showered morning, noon and night. I took up smoking, a universal habit among servicemen in those days.

We worked constantly to stay busy. My plane was a C-130H model, and our job was to refuel Jolly Green Giant helicopters in the air. We flew almost every day, sometimes hauling back bodies of our soldiers and carrying out the grisly work of reassembling limbs of our fallen comrades into body bags. During night flights, we would toss out flares into the dense Vietnam landscape, illuminating the whereabouts of the troops following us. I had no idea what, or who, we were hitting below. Vietcong troops caught in lights had little chance; the coming helicopters would shower them with explosives.

We frequently watched movies on base in the evening to pass the time, settling onto rows of benches with our smokes and a bottle of booze. The films were a welcome escape from life under constant threat and one of the few times we could truly relax. The night was warm and humid, the heavy air lulling us further into complacency.

BOOM!

After a deafening crack that I felt in my stomach, the movie screen burst into flames, small pieces of it catapulting through the air. I leapt off the bench in surprise, dropped my bottle and hit the ground, my arms covering my head and neck as we were taught to do. I could hear the footsteps all around, the ground vibrating with the sounds of hundreds of boots pounding by.

So now my time has come. Thanks, God.

But I wasn't ready to concede. I jumped up and fell in stride with the crazed mass of running men. There was no time to think; only time to run for my life from an unexpected attack.

That night, the movie screen was our only casualty. Someone had thrown a satchel charge at the screen, obliterating it. I tasted the reality of death for the first time and was caught in the sights and sounds of panicked men sprinting for their lives.

The movie screen bombing was little preparation for the scale of our next surprise attack.

I sometimes worked night duty on the plane, performing maintenance and getting it ready for its next flight. Twenty-five planes were lined up wing to wing between the brick walls of a bunker designed to protect them from ground attacks.

Every night, the dark ocean was speckled with the lanterns hanging on Vietnamese dinghies; the local people were out fishing. We grew used to them out there, although we knew that they could beach their boats and come onto our base anytime.

This night, the ocean seemed more lit up than usual, the spots of light bouncing off the waves.

"We're going to get hit tonight," my friends and I muttered, alarmed at the increase in dinghies. There was nothing we could do except go about our work with a sense of dread in our souls.

The first explosion came just after midnight. We had the plane's tailgate down and were loading cargo in from the back. Many planes were full of fuel, enough for its flight and for refueling the Jolly Greens. The Vietcong soldiers ran along the brick walls of the bunker, pulling pins on satchel charges and tossing them into the backs of the planes.

Our base was equipped with a siren that would sound a warning if Vietcong came on base, giving us time to get the planes up and out. That night, it failed.

Our men raced ahead of the Vietcong attackers, shouting and bumping into each other toward safety. Guys fell down who were hurt from the explosions. A plane that was two down from mine burst into flames when the satchel charge hit its fuel tanks. I had never seen a C-130 burn in my life.

The air was cluttered with noise. Guns fired. The siren finally went off. Planes that weren't hit took off into the air to escape the attack. I just ran, picking up guys who were hurt and rushing them to the medical area. The pandemonium disoriented us. Were there more Vietcong swarming on base from the sea?

"Get your a** out of here!" I screamed to a guy who was still by our plane. "Run! Now!"

I caught sight of two drinking buddies nearby. "Is everybody out of that plane?" I yelled, striding past them.

"Everybody's out!" they confirmed. An explosion shook the ground as I ran back to my plane. When I turned to make sure my buddies were clearing out, too, they were gone. Vanished. Blasted to pieces in a single explosion.

When you see your friends blown up in front of you, it has a lasting effect.

The battle raged through the night as we fought to keep control of the base. Vietcong covered it like ants on an anthill, not caring whether they lived or died in the attack. I picked up friends who were hurt, some with limbs blown off, and carried them to safety. To my own surprise, I found myself praying as I ran.

If I go tonight, take care of my brothers and sisters. Let Mom know that her prayers for my safety didn't work, okay?

I prayed the Act of Contrition at least four times. The words I learned in Catholic church as a child filled my head as I stared at death.

O my God,
I am heartily sorry for having offended Thee, and I detest all my sins, because I dread the loss of heaven, and the

pains of hell; but most of all because they offend Thee, my God, Who art all good and deserving of all my love. I firmly resolve, with the help of Thy grace, to confess my sins, to do penance and to amend my life. Amen.

I had been taught in church that when death is certain, if you die with God's name on your lips, you'll go to heaven. As long as I repeated that prayer, I figured I had a 90 percent chance of God taking me straight up to be with him.

But the truth was that I didn't want to die in Vietnam.

Please let me live through this. I know you have other plans for me, God.

As the sun rose over the South China Sea, we finally wrested control of our base back from the Vietcong. They took out five of our planes and a number of men. Miraculously, my body wasn't so much as scratched.

I had never really wanted to be in Vietnam, but now I really wanted out.

I had seen so much death, in such horrible ways, that I was no longer afraid of it. I just hoped that when it was my time, I'd go in my sleep.

Six weeks prior to my discharge in March of 1969, I relieved myself of my command on the plane. I had built up vacation time, but I didn't travel anywhere. I stayed on base and became a regular in the chapel there, which seemed like the safest place I could find. If the Vietcong came for us again, I rationalized, they wouldn't target the chapel.

I prayed to God a lot during those weeks.

When I left the base for good, we were flown to Saigon and spent the night before returning to the United States. A crop of new kids was there waiting to begin their tour in 'Nam. They had climbed to the roof of the hotel and were drinking and carrying on, yelling and shouting like they were in the wee hours of a fraternity party. They had yet to taste the fear and anxiety of serving here.

The night sky lit up, almost like the Fourth of July. A cheer erupted from the new kids, as if they were watching the climactic scene in an action movie. Saigon was being shelled, and the guys were having a grand old time.

I wanted to scream at those kids to get down. They could get killed up there. This was real, not a movie.

Well, God, here's another group for you to take care of. I'm going home.

I tried to resume a normal life in the United States. I married Adele, who was four years younger than me, in 1969, and we went on to have six children. I had seen plenty of love stories in movies, and I wanted someone to take care of me and love me forever. Unlike my hurried, rejected proposal to my high school girlfriend, when I asked Adele to marry me it was out of love. We settled down, and I got a job at a shipyard.

For a while in Vietnam, I'd picked up a pot-smoking habit. But I had left it there, cramming all of my supplies in a coffee tin and tossing it to one of the guys on my way out. Pot numbed my senses and made the worry dissipate. I didn't have a girlfriend or wife waiting for me at home, so I created my own little world in my mind. It was a place where I could escape and dream.

But I didn't give up the drinking when my service ended, and now I drank a lot. Many days, I drank half a case of beer. Pictures kept flashing in my mind of the awful things I'd seen in Vietnam, playing in my head like a horror movie.

Loud sounds scared me, instantly taking me back to the night the Vietcong infiltrated the base. Nighttime thunderstorms sounded like incoming planes. Adele would reach over and grab me as I was jumping out of bed and running for cover. More than once I threw the mattress up and over for protection — with Adele still on it.

At the end of my shift at the shipyard one day, I headed to the locker room to put my things away before I met my dad in the parking lot. Dad, who also worked at the shipyard, got worried when I didn't show up. He found me on a bench next to a row of lockers.

He sat down next to me. "Junior, what's wrong?"

"I don't want to go back there."

"What do you mean?"

Leaving Vietnam

Dad was never very compassionate about emotional problems, and he offered his usual response to my anxiety over life in the outside world.

"You're a man, suck it up." He wasn't interested in listening to my struggles. "You need to get in your car and drive home."

"I can't handle it out there. It's not right. I can't do this." I settled my head into my hands, hardly able to support the weight of the images of Vietnam that plagued my mind.

"C'mon. It's just in your head." He gently tugged on my elbow, and I followed him outside.

For some reason, I could handle the responsibilities of war, but I couldn't handle a wife and child. I was having a nervous breakdown.

Any closeness I'd developed with God in Vietnam returned to distance after I came home. Adele was a strong Catholic, and I attended church with her every Sunday for a while. Eventually, I stopped going because I just wasn't interested anymore. My feelings were numbed, and I didn't want to worry about relating to God anymore. I had talked to God on the beaches of Vietnam and in the skies over jungles. If I was going to have a spiritual life, it didn't need to be confined to church.

The world was colored in black and white for me now.

If there's a God, if he's ready to take me, I'll meet him. If not, the worms will have me.

Adele and I struggled in our marriage. We had six children: three boys and three girls. She was a lot like my father — unsympathetic to my ongoing difficulties stemming from Vietnam. Sometimes she told me that I wasn't a kid anymore, and I needed to grow up.

Adele and I divorced in 1997, but we got back together less than three years later. We worked hard on putting our marriage back together. I moved back into a guest bedroom in our house at first, and after several years, we once again shared a room. My kids were thrilled that we were together again.

In 2008, with our marriage nearly back to normal, Adele went into the hospital for triple bypass surgery. She came through the surgery all right, so I joined her in the ICU to watch a movie that night. I turned the lights off so we could see the screen of the hospital TV better.

Adele was too tired to finish the movie, but I kept watching while she laid her head back on the hospital bed to sleep. The room buzzed and hummed with Adele's monitors, but the sound of air hissing out of the mask of her breathing apparatus startled me.

I jumped up and turned the light on. The mask had slipped off her face, so I repositioned it over her nose and mouth. She didn't stir, so I looked closer. Adele wasn't breathing.

Hospital staff rushed into the room at my call, shocking her with electric pads and pumping her chest to restart her heart. I watched helplessly from the side of the room.

Why, God? I screamed in my head. *Why'd you do this? She and I were working everything out. We were becoming husband and wife again, and you called quits on it.*

I picked up the phone next to Adele's bed and hit redial, calling one of my sons who had been at the hospital with us earlier. I was crying so hard that he couldn't understand anything I was saying.

"Dad," he pleaded, "you're not making any sense."

"Why did God do this? It's just not right." I couldn't find anything else to say, so I repeated myself over and over.

According to the surgeon, Adele had come through the procedure with flying colors. She would have moved out of the ICU the next day, and after a few days in the hospital, she was supposed to come home.

Doctors said it was a freak accident. Adele died two weeks before her birthday and our 41st wedding anniversary.

I was angry and dejected for a long time after Adele's death. I should have been the one to die, not Adele. Together we had 15 grandchildren, and we had loved taking care of them together. Now, I was on my own.

Finally, my three sons decided it was time for me to meet someone new and find some companionship other than my grandchildren, who were always around. When I came home from a friend's house one night, my sons were waiting for me. They sat me down in front of the computer and pulled up an Internet browser.

"Type in this site," one of them told me. It was a dating site for seniors.

Changing Course

All of these women popped up on the screen. I surfed around the site for a while, and eventually I came across Michele. We corresponded for six months before meeting in person.

I took a ferry to our first date. She was Irish, and like Adele, she was hot-tempered and sure of her ways. It only took three dates for me to decide to go after her, even though my emotions still felt frozen.

Michele soon broached the subject of church with me and invited me to a Sunday service at Harbor Life Church in Gig Harbor, Washington.

"I'd love to go," I said, "but I really don't believe much of that anymore. God's never really helped me."

I enjoyed the service. Hearing the pastor talk made me feel relieved and comfortable. He spoke of unity and family, and his words seemed to be spoken just for me. I longed for these things, but after so many unanswered prayers, I thought God wasn't interested in letting me have them. Listening to the pastor sparked hope. Could it be that God wanted to help me open my war-weary heart and love again?

"I really like what the pastor says," I told Michele as we walked outside afterward. "Do you mind if I come back again?"

We became regulars and then members of Harbor Life. I made some new friends, including a man who had lost a wife of many years and recently remarried.

Attending church together brought Michele and I closer, and my heart began opening to her and to God. My emotions had been shell-shocked in Vietnam and were numbed again after Adele's death. My feelings for Michele grew into a true love, an emotion I didn't think I'd feel again. When I said, "I love you" to Michele, I really meant it. I didn't want to lose her.

I felt cheated of Adele, but now God had given me Michele.

We were married in Michele's backyard in 2011. Everything was casual, and my grandkids ran around happily during the ceremony. We laughed when my 2-year-old grandson helped himself to a piece of wedding cake before it was cut.

The morning after our wedding, I turned over and looked at Michele.

"Good morning, Mrs. Tabares." I smiled at my new wife. "God bless you."

Inside, I was alive. Would I ever have a morning as pure and beautiful as this one? It was so easy to hold Michele and say, "I love you." I thanked God for her. I thanked God for giving me back my life and helping me leave the heart-hardening experiences of Vietnam behind.

When I Stopped Trying

The Story of Scott and Nicole Johnson

Written by Jessica Boling

We were fighting again.

"Nicole, why can't you rinse the dishes before you put them in here?" Scott demanded, reaching into the dishwasher and holding up a lasagna-encrusted plate. "The machine can't handle this much junk."

My head throbbed, and I took a deep breath. "If you feel that way, maybe you should do all the dishes yourself."

He shook his head. Turning to the sink, he scrubbed the plate vigorously.

"I can't believe you!" I yelled. "You get upset about everything. What is wrong with you?"

"What is wrong with *me*?" he scoffed. With his back turned, he continued to scrub the plate. "You're the one who's yelling!"

"Oh, really? Well, now you are, too."

Our 6 year old called from the other room, and I went to see what he needed. I knew that Scott and I didn't fight well, but I felt justified in raising my voice when he acted like that. As I helped my son, Carter, with his homework, my anger cooled, and I wondered why Scott and I fought over such petty things: cleaning the house, washing the dishes or taking Carter to school or an event. Deep in my heart, I sensed that there was something wrong with our relationship. It was a familiar feeling.

Changing Course

Scott and I met in college. He was my roommate's brother, and I heard a lot about him before we met. When we did see each other, I was immediately smitten. My outgoing personality attracted him, and I felt magnetically drawn to his quiet demeanor. We dated for two years and married, young and optimistic, in 1993.

My husband's introspective nature was a beautiful mystery, and the first five years of our marriage were harmonious enough. In 1998, I gave birth to our son, Carter. He had club feet and needed casts for the first year of his life, and he also had severe reflux that kept him constantly wailing.

As mothering duties screamed for my attention, Scott receded quietly to the background. A few months after Carter's birth, I realized that although I was married, I felt alone. The dawning of such a feeling swept a cold chill through my heart.

For the first time, I doubted that I could improve my relationship with Scott. I'd thought I could fix him — thought that if I just loved him enough, nurtured him enough and encouraged him enough, he would be free from the memories that haunted him.

We rarely talked about it, but I knew. Before I met Scott, his sister Michele — my college roommate — told me.

"Nicole," she said, "my brother has something in his past. Something really terrible."

"What?" I asked. Although I hadn't met him, I was curious.

Michele took a deep breath and looked at the floor. "He was raped. By a man in our church."

My stomach turned. "Really? When?"

"A long time ago. When he was a kid."

"But your dad is the pastor." I realized that didn't make any difference and wished I hadn't said it.

"Yeah, he is. And he knows about it, of course, and dealt with it."

Because Michele told me about the situation before I met her brother, I had time to digest the information first. I felt sick with indignation at what he had been through, and my compassion was ripe by the time I laid eyes on the quiet, retiring college guy. When we were dating and newly married, we talked occasionally about his past, but it did not seem to affect our relationship. I loved him, and he loved me. We committed our lives to each other in marriage, and I hoped we'd live happily ever after, with Scott's past experiences receding into distant history. If I loved him enough and cared for him well, I was sure the healing would happen.

Eleven years later, we were fighting over trivial household issues. Carter was 6 years old, and I was seven months pregnant with our second child. Scott lived with me, ate with me and slept with me, but I felt completely disconnected from him. We fought because our emotional connection was broken — ripped in half by his aloofness and my frustration. He had closed the door to me, and the more I knocked on it, the more he retreated to the safety of quietness and brooding. And sleeping.

I could taste the tension between us. Scott sat on the couch, his eyes half-closed, arms limp by his sides. I watched him sigh deeply, glance one more time at me and close his eyes.

Trying to stop my heart from hammering, I leaned against a chair and rubbed my round belly. Between the pregnancy, caring for our son and worrying about my husband, I was exhausted. And despite Scott's presence in the room, I felt lonely.

"Scott," I said, measuring my words. "We need to talk."

He opened his eyes but didn't move.

I crossed the room and sat on the couch. Carefully, I weighed my words before speaking. This couldn't become another shouting match. Carter was asleep in the next room, and besides, I wanted a real conversation. I knew what I had to say, and when I spoke, my voice was soft and even.

"What is it?" he asked, closing his eyes again.

"Scott, I've told you many times that I'd like you to get help. I hate seeing you like this. You're depressed."

"I know," he said, eyes still closed. "So what can I do about it? I don't see how counseling is going to change that."

"I need you to get help for your depression, or I am going to have to make some changes."

Scott's eyes opened. He turned to meet my gaze.

"Are you threatening me?" he asked.

"No, I'm not threatening you." I swallowed, trying to quiet my heart. "I'm just telling you what I have to do. I need you to be committed to our marriage. If you're not, I need to take steps to do something different."

He put his arm around me and buried his face in my shoulder.

"I am committed," he said. And I knew he meant it.

"Scott," I blinked away tears, determined to finish what I needed to say, "I'm already trying to change myself, but I need you to try, too. I don't think God wants you to feel this shame, either. I want you to get better." I paused. "I love you deeply."

"I love you, too, honey." He embraced me, and we cried together.

It was a turning point. After that conversation, I knew he was committed. Relief flooded my heart. I stopped thinking about separating and began thinking about how we could work things out.

Daily, sometimes hourly, I begged God to do something to fix my husband, to take away Scott's unbearable pain. I saw him isolating himself from others, drawing back in distrust and avoiding friendships with other men. As a teenager, counseling had helped me recover from unhealthy relationships. I sought it again as an adult to help me deal with a food addiction. I knew that counseling worked for me, and I wanted it to work for Scott. Since I couldn't fix his problems, perhaps someone else could.

Changing Course

Stewing about our many issues, I struggled to understand and accept my life. I wanted to do something to make it better. When I craved control and my craving went unsatisfied, I was glad to have faith to lean on. At church camp as a kid, I sought out an enthusiastic young counselor who showed me how to talk to God. I savored the personal attention from an adult, but my decision to get to know God only lasted through the weeklong camp. Later, at age 13, I made a deeper commitment. I was attracted to Jesus because in church I learned that even though he was God's son, he experienced life as a person like me so I could relate to him. I wanted to learn about him and to handle life more like him. Although raging hormones and conflicting emotions led me to seek attention from boys during my teenage years, simultaneously the idea of a loving God drew me back to Jesus. I grew up with a single mom, and the image of God as my father, a figure that I craved but never had, pulled me with magnetic force.

One day I was praying again that Scott would seek counseling and that it would be the answer we needed to heal our marriage. Suddenly, I saw a clear picture in my mind.

Scott stood in our church, at the front of the auditorium. He was not alone. People gathered around him. Their hands were outstretched, touching his head and shoulders. Scott's head was bowed, his eyes closed. The people around him — our friends and neighbors from the church — lowered their heads in similar posture, and one after another they spoke aloud, asking God to heal Scott's heart.

I shook off the mental picture, wondering what it meant. After considering it, I wondered if God could be communicating to me that he wanted to heal Scott in a different way than I expected.

A few weeks later, another mental picture popped into my head. In it, I saw Scott sitting in our pastor's office and sharing openly about his depression and its roots in the sexual abuse he endured as a child. Again I saw heads bowed in prayer as the pastor spoke words of faith over Scott, asking God to heal the hurt and remove the shame.

These images puzzled me, but I continued to pray and I realized that God might answer in a different way than I expected.

Scott did pursue counseling, but his depression continued for several years. Our daughter, Beatrice, was born, Scott's construction business thrived and we managed to maintain our commitment to each other. All the time, I continued to pray for our marriage because I knew it could be much better.

Suddenly, Scott's past was not the only challenge we faced. The economic downturn began to seriously affect the construction business Scott owned with his brother and father.

When he arrived home from work one afternoon, I

could see panic in his eyes. I sent the children to another room to play and closed the door behind them.

"What is it?"

"Nicole, I can't believe what's happening. We could barely make this month's mortgage payments on the houses we built, and they are depreciating in value every day they don't sell."

I clenched my fists and took a breath, trying to quell the anxiety rising in my chest. For years, Scott's company had built numerous houses and sold them for reasonable rates. Satisfied customers referred their friends, and the company had a good reputation for quality work and fair prices.

But now, good work and low prices did nothing to attract buyers. The housing market was collapsing around our shoulders, and every week brought the company — and our family — closer to bankruptcy.

"Isn't there something we can do?" I asked. As always, I felt the undeniable urge to do something to fix the situation.

"Yes, but I didn't want it to happen." Scott's hunched shoulders and lowered eyes painted a visible picture of defeat.

"The house?"

He nodded silently. "We're losing the house."

Our house. I looked around the large living room, replete with big-screen television and plush couches. I had never wanted this house, but Scott had. He called it our "grown-up" house. I thought it was a mansion, too large for our needs, but I had grown attached to it in the few years since we'd moved. Now we were losing it.

And we didn't have our older smaller home to return to, because we were losing that house, too.

"Where will we go?" I asked after hearing that we would lose both houses. "Where will we live?"

"My parents have offered to let us stay with them," he said. "If we all pitch in, we can help them keep their house, at least." His parents owned a large home much like ours. There would be plenty of room for all of us there. Despite the unexpected blow, I felt secure knowing that my children would have a roof over their heads.

Scott and I were silent for a full minute, soaking in the situation.

"Well," I said at last, moving toward the door, "I guess I should start packing."

Scott didn't respond. Over the next several days, we began making piles of our possessions and loading them into boxes. The children helped with taping and labeling. Their sadness to leave our house was replaced almost immediately with excitement. They loved their grandparents, and the idea of all of us living together filled them with delight. Childish exuberance might have thrived in one half of our family, but Scott and I felt the full weight of our situation.

I strived to hold things together, working all day as a nurse, picking up the kids from school, making dinner and packing the boxes in preparation for our move. As I battled my own anxiety, I watched Scott spiral into a new depth of depression. When I left for work in the morning, he was asleep. When I returned with the kids in the afternoon, I found him in bed with his eyes closed.

"Honey, are you all right?" I asked, afraid to know the answer.

He opened his eyes briefly, and I could see the despair emanating from their depths. I was looking into the eyes of a man who had given up on life.

"I'm sorry. It's my fault." His voice was low, broken.

"It's not your fault," I said, sitting beside him. "It's not. The economy is failing. Thousands of people are out of work. It's everywhere, Scott, and it's affecting everyone — not just us. You didn't cause this."

He shook his head, refusing to believe me.

The week before we moved, Scott came downstairs while I was cooking dinner and said he was having chest pains. Immediately, I drove him to the hospital, where they decided to keep him overnight to run tests.

The next day, after dropping off the kids at school and heading to work, I received a phone call from the hospital.

"Your husband has had an episode," said the nurse. "He's okay, but you'd better come now."

I excused myself from work and jumped into the car. When I reached the hospital, I rode the elevator to the correct floor, impatient to know what was going on. Halfway down the hall to Scott's room, I saw him approaching from the other direction. A nurse pushed him in a wheelchair.

When I Stopped Trying

"Scott!" I rushed toward him, and my stomach twisted with anxiety. He looked incredibly pale — ghastly, half-dead, with eyes sunken into the thin frame of his face. How had my husband gone from bad to worse in such a short amount of time? "Oh, God, what happened to you?" I asked.

The nurse explained that Scott's doctor ordered the treadmill stress test that morning. Scott had done very well on the test; all his readings were normal, and the monitors had detected no blockages in his heart or other arteries.

"When I got off the treadmill, they told me everything was great," Scott found strength to explain. "But I didn't *feel* great. I felt horrible. I felt a roaring in my ears, and my vision started to go. I passed out."

"His heart rate dropped to 30 beats per minute," said the nurse. "But we resuscitated him."

"Thirty beats per minute?" I repeated. As a nurse, I knew the severity of such a reading. The truth smacked me squarely in the face: My husband had almost died.

After the nurse settled Scott in his room and satisfied herself with his heart monitor's reading, she left me with him. I sat by the bed and held his hand.

"It felt like I was at the back of a dark cave," he said, closing his eyes and recalling what he had experienced that morning. "Then when they gave me the shot and revived me, I had the sensation of moving forward. When I woke up, I felt worse than I had before I passed out."

I squeezed his hand. "And how do you feel now?"

"Grateful." Scott was always a man of few words, but

this word carried with it all the sincerity of one who has been given a new beginning — a second chance at life.

Later, Scott confessed that in the days before his chest pains, he had been planning to take his own life. Stress and anxiety compounded by depression and unhealed hurt from the past drove him to contemplate a desperate act. He hadn't wanted to leave us alone or grieve us in any way. He had only wanted to end the pain that gnawed, relentlessly, at his mind and his heart.

"And to think I almost got what I wanted." He shook his head. "It wasn't what I wanted. I'm so glad I didn't die. I'm so *grateful*." He looked at me, and for the first time in years, I saw a spark of hope in his eyes. Although I struggled to understand how, I knew that something had changed in my husband's heart. Changed for the better.

Only a week after Scott's near-death experience in the hospital, our family moved in with his parents. Closing the large front door of our empty house and driving away from it for the last time should have been a painful experience, I thought — but to me it was a joyful one. Day after day, I sensed improvement in my husband's outlook and in our marriage. We were communicating again, sharing thoughts and emotions more freely than we had done in years. While the economy plunged to new depths, our relationship rose from the rubble of the collapsed construction business. I continued to pray, this time with gratitude for what I saw God beginning to do, and our marriage continued to heal.

In October 2009, nine months after he nearly died in the hospital, Scott stood in front of our congregation at Harbor Life Church and told his story. He told them about the abuse he'd suffered, about the depression that had nearly crushed him and about the contemplated suicide. He told them about almost losing his life and about finding it again in the hospital, weak and weary from years of mental anguish.

"And you know what?" he asked everyone. "After a thorough checkup, the doctor said nothing is wrong with my heart. The only thing that was wrong with me that day was I was stressed. Stressed beyond belief. So I'm here to tell you that stress really can kill you."

A few people laughed, but they took the information seriously. From my chair near the front of the room, I listened as Scott told of his gratefulness to be alive and of the peace that he felt.

"I am not only grateful to be alive," he said. "I'm grateful that I went through the experience of nearly losing my life. God knew it was what I needed to wake up. I wouldn't trade that experience for anything, because I know what the results have been. My heart is healing, my marriage is healing and I finally feel at peace. I've always wanted to be at peace with whatever happens, but I could never achieve that. It drove me crazy. But now, I am at peace. I don't have to bear responsibility or shame for what someone did to me years ago, or even for decisions I made about the business, or mistakes I made in my marriage to Nicole. Jesus does that. He gives me peace."

He smiled, and his face transformed. My heart swelled with love and pride.

After he told his story, the pastor asked people to gather around Scott and pray for him. As many people moved toward the front of the room, I experienced a feeling of déjà vu and gasped. *This is it. People standing around him, praying for him.* It was the mental picture I'd seen nearly five years before, becoming a reality.

Only a few weeks later, Scott and I were sitting in the pastor's office for a counseling session. Scott shared more details of his story, and the pastor offered to pray for us. I realized that the second mental picture I'd received five years previously was also coming true.

On April 4, 2011, I gave birth to a healthy little boy. Our third child, Tyson, was a symbol of new life and renewal in our marriage.

One day when Tyson was a few months old, I sat cuddling him on the couch, gazing into his deep blue eyes. Scott came home from work, and the two older children tackled him immediately. After a few minutes, they returned to their play, and he came over to share the couch with me.

"I'm sorry the house is a mess," I said, looking at the toys strewn across the floor and remembering the dirty dishes in the sink.

"It's okay," Scott said, and I knew he meant it. He kissed me and placed an arm gently around my shoulders. We both stared into Tyson's eyes, entranced.

I leaned against him and thanked God for giving me back my husband; the one I loved so dearly. Hard as I'd tried, I couldn't fix Scott's problems — or my problems. I couldn't create the healing that I desperately wanted. But Jesus could.

And when I stopped trying to fix us, he did.

Out of the Dark

The Story of Paul

Written by Karen Russell Holmes

It was the 70s, but our neighborhood could have been plucked from a 1950s television show. Stucco mission homes with one-car garages along tree-lined streets suggested idyllic family lives to match. Unlike our well-manicured lawns, our lives were not so neat and tidy.

Sitting in his breakfast nook, my best friend, John, and I were rolling reds and whites in aluminum foil for his drug-dealer brother, Sam, while their parents were at work. Sam was big and much older than us. He had a mean streak that neither John nor I wanted to face.

"Hurry up and get it done before the old man gets back, you little squirts," Sam barked.

We had rolled pills for Sam many times before, and I didn't fear getting caught anymore. My only fear was Sam, who dealt drugs in several states and eventually did prison time for it. He was big time for our little part of Los Angeles.

Drugs were not the only secret locked behind our perfect front doors. John's hid an alcoholic mother and stepfather; mine hid monsters, which I met when I was 4.

Trying to help me conquer my fear of the dark, my father took my hand and led me down the lightless hall from my bedroom to the den. The 10-foot walk to the light switch in the den seemed endless.

"It's okay, son," my father encouraged me. "There is nothing here that can hurt you."

We repeated the exercise on many occasions, but I only made it by myself once.

Afterward, he would throw me over his shoulder like a sack of wheat. I giggled all the way as he bounced me to my room and dumped me on my bed for my mom to tuck me in.

"Remember, there's no such thing as monsters. There's nothing to be afraid of," he said, turning off the light.

These are the last memories I have of his undivided attention and assurance that all was well. By the time I entered school, Dad became a hands-off father, like many men of his generation.

Of course, Dad didn't have nurturing parents to teach him. Every Sunday, we went to his parents' house to watch *Walt Disney's Wonderful World of Color*. They were the only people we knew with a color TV!

But instead of cuddling in their arms while engrossed in the program, we were told to sit quietly by ourselves. Instead of lingering after the show to discuss school, friends or hobbies, my grandparents popped up from their seats and ushered us to the front door as soon as the program was over.

Dad wasn't there to guide me down the hall or plop me on the bed with reassurances anymore. And I soon found out he was wrong. There were monsters, after all. Hideous figures walked the hall nightly from my brother's room to mine as I dove under the covers, trembling. One loomed in my doorway, and I dared to charge past it, screaming, to the safety of my parents' room.

I was scared to go to bed every night. My mom would take me to bed, and I would have to know exactly where she was going to be before I would lie down. If one of these wicked things walked into my room, I needed to know where she was.

"Okay, I'm going to be in the den and then maybe in the kitchen because I'm probably going to get a snack," she reassured me.

According to my parents, the dim nightlight warded off monsters. My dad, being quite miserly, had chosen the lowest wattage light in order to save money. (He timed our showers when we got older.) If this light was not enough, then tough.

As terrifying as the monsters were, it did not keep me from looking further into darker experiences. As I got older, I became fascinated with gory things. I bought books about the supernatural and learned to cast spells. By the time I was 9, my parents suspected something, though I tried to hide my growing interest in the dark side.

"Paul, where are you?" Mom called down the hallway. "Supper's ready."

"Uh, don't come in here," I said, panicking. "I'll come in just a minute."

In blind haste, I scurried to shove the books between my mattress and box springs.

"What are you doing in there?" Mom queried. "You have been acting so strange lately."

Changing Course

I had opened Pandora's Box, and the occult quickly became my obsession. I learned to use a Ouija board and, by the time I was 13, was in regular communication with a spiritual entity. My parents would hear me late at night talking to no one in my room.

"Who do you suppose he's talking to?" Mom worried.

"I don't know," Dad retorted angrily. "Paul, be quiet! It's the middle of the night, and I have an early morning." Later in life, they told me they thought I had gone mad and almost took me to a psychiatrist.

While in junior high school, I met some other boys who shared my search for meaning through dark religion. Together, we delved deeper into this inky world. Whenever I tried to convince my parents that this was more than fun and games, they tuned me out.

Until one day, as we sat around the kitchen table having breakfast, my parents learned we were not alone. *Whiz!* A sizeable ceramic bowl flew off the top of the refrigerator. If my mother hadn't caught it in mid-air, it would have hit my father in the face.

"What was that?" they exclaimed.

"I've been trying to tell you," I said. Speechless, we finished our breakfast.

I was proud in that moment. There had been stuff moving around my room for quite some time. This occurrence in front of my parents would validate me with them, or so I thought. But it only made things worse as my parents nagged me daily. "What is wrong with you?" they demanded. "Why can't you be normal?"

Unlike the terrifying monsters that haunted me in childhood, I took comfort in this peaceful visitor. I wasn't immune to fear by any means, but since I couldn't actually *see* it, I imagined it angelic. It lulled me into the sense that it was taking care of me. When I went out to sell drugs, I thought that I would not get caught because my invisible friend was watching over me. It filled the void I felt from missing a deeper relationship with my father. It came when I called and left when I asked. I was in control.

I tried to talk to my brother about it once when, all of a sudden, he bolted out of his chair, shouting, "It's right behind me, isn't it?!"

Yep. I'd been aware of it the whole time we talked. My brother had finally felt its presence, too.

"Make it leave," my brother insisted. I told it to leave, and it did.

A spooky throng of costumed people haunted the local park for a Halloween dance. Some of them were there for old-fashioned family fun. Others came to party, though not in the open. At 13, I was there with the partiers.

Music pulsated through open windows into the musty bathroom. My brother's friend passed me an opium pipe under the smoke-filled bathroom stall he occupied.

"Sure, why not," I said confidently, drawing a deep drag, hoping he wouldn't notice it was my first time.

I wasn't content to package drugs for Sam. I imagined

dealers had power and prestige and soon joined their ranks. Driven — in pursuit of admiration and importance — I became the go-to guy for anything a drug user could want. Sure, I made money, but I'd give away most of my own stash at parties for attention.

One night when I was 15, the police showed up at my door. I was in my bedroom with a sizeable bag of LSD under my bed when the narcotics detectives told my parents they were there to talk to me.

"We understand that you are affiliated with certain kids at school," one of the detectives said, rattling off their names.

"I only know them from gym class," I lied.

"That's good enough for me," my mom said. "Now get out," she told the cops. My mother was a free spirit, and she was the nurturer in the family, so that confrontation was out of character for her. She was a stay-at-home mom who babied us by making our beds and doing everything for us. If lima beans were sitting on my plate and I had refused to eat them, when my dad left the room, she took them and stuffed them in a potato skin and threw them away. If I said I didn't know the troublemakers the police named, well, that was good enough for her.

"How dare you lie to Mom like that," my brother rebuked me later.

"You should talk. You're driving around with a roach clip hanging from your mirror," I retorted.

How dare he? I thought. He was just as much a drug user as me.

Out of the Dark

As my drug use escalated, so did my health problems. I was placed in a special education gym class because I lacked the stamina to keep up with the regular classes. I couldn't run a quarter mile without losing my breath. Eventually my parents took me to a cardiologist in Los Angeles.

Reading my test results, the specialist announced, right in front of my mother, "You're doing drugs."

Of course, I denied it.

"This is exactly the type of damage I see in heroin addicts," he continued.

I never did heroin, but the results were evidence of the host of other drugs I'd been using. The doctor advised bypass surgery due to a blockage, but my parents weren't sold. I mean, come on, who'd ever heard of bypass surgery for someone my age? I played on their doubt, insisting I was fine. I convinced myself, too, and continued my lifestyle of drugs and darkness.

"Can I score some dope from you?" Al asked outside the classroom door.

"What do you want?" I asked.

"A joint."

"Just one?"

"Yeah."

I entered the empty classroom and rolled him a joint at my desk. Since I didn't know him, I rolled up pencil shavings instead of pot as a prank. He enjoyed the prank, and a friendship was forged.

My new friend was a practicing Hindu and prided himself on a dark, mysterious personality. Still driven in pursuit of meaning and truth, I sought to learn all I could about Al's religion. I quit drugs to have a clear mind in order to study Hinduism.

Al and I attended a Hindu temple in Northern Pasadena filled with wealthy older women from nearby wealthy neighborhoods. I strictly obeyed the swami's instructions, learning the main tenants of the religion and how to meditate. I spent most of my time trying to become one with a candle that flickered in the meditation room. It never happened.

Okay, what was next? Taoism. I began to study this philosophy on my own, but it was hard to process. This belief system was established to stop warring factions in China. The idea was that if desire were eliminated from a person, the need to fight would also be gone. So now I was trying to become one with a great nameless uncarved block of wood. Wood has no desires, therefore becoming one with the block of wood would somehow strip me of all my desire. This went on for a year.

In a search for more truth, I joined a group on a trip to Joshua Tree National Park to commune with nature when I was 17. I loved being alone outdoors, so the park's 550,000 acres of wilderness appealed to me. We set up camp and began our usual ritual of meditation over several days. Someone in the group found Jimsonweed —

a poisonous hallucinogenic plant. The group brewed and drank it to get high, though I did not. For days, I watched their fruitless efforts to become one in this altered state.

One morning as the sun dawned over the horizon, I sat in my tent, meditating, when I thought, *This is all just a bunch of crap! I'm not getting any closer to finding meaning than these fools I am with who are hallucinating together in the desert. This isn't truth.*

I walked out onto the sun-scorched desert a short distance by myself. Hopeless and disillusioned, I looked to the sky. "Am I reaching you?" I begged. "I want to know the truth."

Flash! From the corner of my eye, I saw a giant orange burst of flame. I turned and saw no fire, but a three-foot high bush that wasn't there before. There were no other bushes in sight in this wasteland. It reminded me of a Bible story I had learned as a small boy. In the story, Moses meets God at a burning bush. Since I had not used any drugs for a year, I was certainly not hallucinating. I knew the God of the Bible was answering me.

"You know what the truth is," spoke a voice so real it was almost audible. That was it! I did know the truth. Without a doubt, God had just shown me.

"I'm out of here," I said, as I packed my gear and left.

As soon as I got home, I told my friend what happened in the desert wilderness. "You need to go with me to a Bible study at Jim's house," she said.

Jim was once a drug-crazed guy who ran naked down the street. But he was different since he became one of those Jesus followers. *I guess if God could change Jim, he could change me, too,* I thought.

"Yeah, I'll go to the study with you," I consented.

I scanned the faces sitting in Jim's living room and felt out of place. I didn't know many of these people and most were older than me. But once the conversation started, I forgot my awkwardness and drank in every word. Jim and the others talked about God like they knew him personally — like he was right there in the room with us. Jim described how every person is created to know God. *That must be it!* I thought. *I've been chasing after things to satisfy a craving, and that craving was for God!* He pointed out what was already obvious to me — that we're all just screw-ups who don't deserve the time of day from God. He told me God would forgive me for being such a screw-up my whole life. All I needed to do was ask him to forgive me and believe that God sent Jesus to die in my place for all the wrong things I'd ever done, he said. God would fill that empty space inside and change me. *Yes,* I thought. *Yes, I want that.*

The now less intimidating guests mingled around the room after the lesson. Jim leaned toward me from his cushioned armchair. "Do you want to know God like this?" he said, smiling.

"Yes!" He didn't have to ask me twice.

"Then pray with me." He bowed his head.

I repeated his words: "God, I'm sorry. I've done so many wrong things. I've hurt others, and I've hurt myself with the lifestyle I've led. Please forgive me. Please help me change, and give my life meaning. Thank you for what Jesus did so I can know you. Help me know you more each day."

"What are you doing? I want those records!" my brother appealed as I cracked each of my record albums in two.

"These records have really bad music on them," I hotly explained. "If God doesn't want me listening to them, he certainly doesn't want you listening to them."

"Boys, what is going on in here?" my dad yelled as he entered my room. The argument escalated with the continued snap of vinyl. "If your brother wants those records, then give them to him. You can't run everyone's life."

This kind of misdirected zeal waned after a couple of years, but I was still eager to share about how God was changing me. At first, I continued to go to parties because I wanted to tell my friends there about Jesus.

One night I was on the way to a party with friends when someone lit a joint in the car. When I passed up my turn for a hit, one guy pointed at me and said, "You're a Jesus freak!" I had said nothing yet about what had happened to me.

Who was this Jesus that he could change a person so much that it simply just showed on him?

Another time, Al and I got a ride to a party with a high priest of the satanic church. While riding along in his old beater, I told them what I learned about Jesus. The guy swerved so dangerously I stopped talking for fear we would crash. I had to find a different way home because he refused to drive me back.

For about a year after that first night at Bible study, signs of my former occult obsession lingered. By the time I got home from Bible study, it was late at night, and my parents were always asleep. As I entered the house through the mudroom, I often heard voices. They stopped when I opened the door to the kitchen.

When I prayed in my bedroom, scratching began on the window screens, and pounding sounded from the walls.

"God, I need to ask," *scratch, scratch, scratch* on the screen, "your forgiveness for yelling at Mom today." *Thud, thud, thud* on the wall behind me. "Please help me be kind to her." *Tap, tap, tap* on the floor.

"I'm stopping. Please stop!" I would shout, each time terrified.

Jim and my new Bible study friends prayed with me about this for almost a year before it stopped. God answered other prayers, too.

"This can't be right," said the cardiologist who had recommended bypass surgery years earlier. He was puzzled. The blockage I had at 15 was not something that would work its way out with time, he said. Yet all tests showed it was gone. At his insistence, I got a second opinion. The second cardiologist confirmed the results. God had healed my heart! My new friends had been praying for that, and now it actually happened!

❧❧❧

Standing at the edge of the church pew, I pushed my long hippie hair off my shoulders and stood up straight. I loved being an usher because I could see everyone as I passed the offering plate from one row to the next. As I glanced down the next row to prepare for the next hand off, a pretty young woman caught my eye. I wanted to talk to her after the church service, but I was too shy.

Once again, God gave me a second chance. My heart jumped, and I couldn't hold back a grin when she walked into Jim's Bible study that week. And, boy, did we talk! We didn't want our conversation to end when everyone filed out of the front door. Our intense courtship continued, and we were married.

At one point in my married life, I inherited some things from my grandmother, including items that once belonged to my great aunt, a spiritualist. The night we brought them home, my wife woke up to see a glowing orb floating in the corner of our bedroom. Without hesitation, she prayed. "God, protect this house, Paul and me from this evil I'm feeling. In Jesus' name, get out of my house now!" The orb disappeared. We knew instantly that we needed to sort through the inheritance and get rid of the things that belonged to my great aunt. The apparition never returned.

Neither have the dark monsters of my childhood. Morning sunlight floods the kitchen where my wife and I hold hands across the table. There is no bowl of pills on the table to package, only our Bibles and coffee cups. There are no frightening, disembodied voices — only the soothing sound of my wife's voice as she bows her head to pray for our day. Together, we thank God for his peace in our home. And I thank him for reaching into my dark world to pull me into his light.

Home Is Where the Heart Is

The Story of Vykki Miller

Written by Karen Koczwara

My heart dropped when I saw my husband's ashen face. "Vykki, I need to talk to you," he said gravely, his voice barely above a whisper. "Your mom just called."

"What is it?" I asked, concern rising in my chest as he pulled me into the other room.

"It's Brandon. He … I'm so sorry … I'm so sorry …"

"What about Brandon?" At the mention of my precious nephew's name, I felt sick. "What is it, Joe?" My voice rose to a shriek.

"He … he passed away last night," Joe managed to say.

"What? Brandon? He's … dead?!" I crumpled to the floor as heavy sobs wracked my body. How could Brandon be dead? He was supposed to be here in two days! We had planned his trip for weeks, plotting the many adventures we'd have together. This couldn't be happening!

"Vykki, I'm so sorry." Joe's eyes filled with tears as he knelt beside me, shaking his head in disbelief. "I can't believe it myself. He was only 16, just a kid."

"What happened? Tell me what happened!" I was hysterical now, gasping for breath as I tried to process the reality.

"He was at a party and drank too much. The doctors called it pulmonary edema. His lungs filled up with fluid when he didn't wake up to cough."

Changing Course

"Stop! Just stop!" My heart couldn't handle any more. I curled into a ball, hanging my head between my knees and shaking uncontrollably as the sobs came from a place deep inside. Peaches and Cream. That was our silly nickname, shortened to the less embarrassing "Peaches" now that he was nearly an adult. So much life, and now he was gone too soon. It wasn't right!

"Noooo!" The groan escaped my lips, erupting from a foreign place inside I didn't know existed. And just like that, a gaping hole formed in its place. A hole I was not sure could ever be filled again.

My story began in North Hollywood, land of movie stars, flashy convertibles, palm trees and glamour. But a red-carpet life was not in my script. Instead, life in the small town would be my fate. And it would be years before I'd truly find my way home.

I was born in 1976; my father was 48 with a head of grey hair, my parents having married later in life. My mother had three children from a previous marriage: a sister nine years my senior and two older brothers.

Two years after my birth, another brother came along. We made our home in a small house with a large swimming pool that provided endless hours of summer fun.

When I was 5 years old, a family friend came to visit. "Why don't you show him your coloring books while we get dinner ready?" my mother suggested, pulling my art supplies out of a drawer.

"Okay," I agreed, grabbing my beloved box of Crayola crayons. Being so much younger than my siblings, I was always grateful for a playmate.

My mother's friend followed me into the other room, where I spread my coloring books out on the table and carefully selected my favorite colors. "How old are you now, Vykki?" he asked, smiling. He had a nice smile, and I decided we might be good friends.

"I'm almost 6," I replied cheerfully as I filled in the thick black lines on the pages.

My head bowed as I concentrated on my work; I scarcely noticed as he inched toward me until his scratchy legs brushed up against mine. Suddenly, I felt his hands somewhere they didn't belong. I didn't know much at 5, but something about this didn't feel right. I tried to scoot away, but he slid his hands farther, making me wiggle uncomfortably. "Please stop that," I whispered, setting my crayon down.

"Aww, it's okay," he murmured, smiling again. But this time, it wasn't a nice smile.

I jumped up and ran down the hall, locking my bedroom door behind me. When my mother called me for dinner, I cowered under the bed covers, afraid to come out. I hoped I'd never see that man again.

When it came time to start kindergarten, I was excited. Having three older siblings, I knew the drill well. When the teacher called us in to sit down at our desks, most of the children burst into tears. But I happily waved to my mother, ready to begin my schooling adventure. At home, however, my nightmare continued.

One evening, we went to the home of my mother's best friend and her husband for dinner. My mother spent nearly every day with her best friend, and I was used to their company. After dinner, the adults pulled out a couple bottles of wine and sent me to a spare bedroom to sleep. "Goodnight, Vykki!" they called out as I padded down the hall.

I had just settled into my bed and had almost drifted off to sleep when I heard soft footsteps in the room. I opened my eyes, assuming my mother had snuck in for one last goodnight kiss. But instead, I saw her friend's husband striding toward me in the darkness. The bed creaked as he sat down beside me. I lay frozen, pretending to be asleep.

Without saying a word, he pushed the covers back and slid his hands up my nightgown. I could smell booze on his breath, his face just inches from mine as he touched me. "Mommy!" I whimpered. "Mommy!"

"Shhh, now, Mommy's having fun out there and doesn't hear you," he slurred, continuing to touch me in places I didn't like at all.

Down the hall, I heard my mother's jolly laugh. I had always loved my mother's laugh, but now, lying here in the darkness with this man I'd thought was her friend, I suddenly hated that laugh. How could they be having so much fun just a few rooms away while this happened?

"Good girl," he murmured. I cringed, squeezing my eyes shut so I didn't have to see his face. At last, he stood up and shuffled out of the room, closing the door quietly behind him. I lay there, listening to my mother's laugh trill down the hall, wishing I could make this night go away, make those people go away, make the shivers that ran down my spine disappear.

The man who colored with me returned on several more occasions, and each time my mother stepped out of the room, he touched me in the same way. "Now, don't tell anyone or I'll hurt your family," he whispered into my ear.

I nodded, terrified. I wanted to tell my mother, but what if he really hurt her? It would be all my fault.

When I was 7, we moved to a smaller town east of Los Angeles. My older siblings were now grown and stayed in the city. The small desert town offered affordable housing and a slower pace of life, but more importantly, it was far away from the men who had hurt me. I enjoyed my new school, but I was terribly shy and had a difficult time making friends. Boys were especially scary; I wanted nothing to do with them. I stuck close by my parents' side and played with my Barbie dolls on our 2-acre property, dragging long roads with the back of shovels and creating detailed cities for them in the dirt. In Barbie Land, everyone was happy.

On occasional Sundays, I donned my best dress and attended the local Catholic church with my parents. The priest stood before us in a shiny robe, reading a series of verses from the Bible in a deep monotone voice. The God he talked about seemed scary and strict with all his rules. If we broke them, the priest explained, we'd be punished forever.

Attending church felt a bit like attending an aerobics class. We stood, kneeled, sat and stood again, then crossed ourselves and filed to the front of the church to take communion. I glanced around the room, watching others to make sure I was doing all the steps right. Trying to make God happy seemed like a lot of work. I decided I didn't much care for church and didn't much care for God.

"Do we have to go to church?" I whined to my father when the next holiday arrived. "It's so boring!"

"God wants us to go every Sunday, not just on special occasions," my father insisted. But eventually, to my relief, he relented and stopped trying to make us all go.

When Christmastime arrived, my mother reminded us why we celebrated the season. "It's Jesus' birthday, remember?"

I nodded. I had spent the past few years piecing together what little I knew about God: We could read about him in a big leather Bible filled with lots of "thee's" and "thou's," he had lots of rules and we weren't supposed to question him.

"Don't forget to thank God for all your blessings," my mother often reminded me, repeating the words of our priest. I knew I had much to be thankful for, but thanking a God I didn't know felt a lot like thanking a stranger. Was there really more to this God than a few random rules?

Home Is Where the Heart Is

When I was 14, my friend invited me to her church youth group. Since I wasn't too fond of my church experience, I hesitated to oblige. "Come on, it will be fun! We play games and sing songs, and there's even a few cute boys there, too," she added with a giggle.

I didn't care about boys. I tried hard to avoid them wherever I went. But the games sounded fun, and besides, there wasn't much to do in our small town on a Friday night. The kids who attended youth group tended to be positive and stayed out of trouble. "Okay, I'll go," I finally agreed.

When we arrived at the church, the youth leader separated us into groups for a game. "Vykki, that's your name, right? You're going to pair up with Alex here," the leader instructed, prodding me toward a boy about my age.

As Alex strode toward me, an awkward smile on his face, I panicked and ran out of the room. When the youth leader found me a few minutes later, he looked concerned. "You okay?" he asked. "Games not really your thing?"

I tried to smile, but inside, my stomach twisted. "Yeah, not really my thing," I mumbled.

I continued to attend youth group and was intrigued by the messages. The youth leader spoke about God as someone who wanted to have a relationship with us. It was quite a contrast to the God I'd envisioned growing up. During game time, I huddled with the girls, always avoiding the boys across the room. One evening the youth pastor stopped by my house to speak with my parents.

They talked in hushed tones across the room, their faces serious. When he left, my parents sat me down.

"Vykki, the youth leader raised some concerns about you tonight," my mother began. "He noticed how fearful you are of the opposite sex and recommended counseling. I think you should go."

My heart beat quickly. Though I'd tried hard to wipe the images from my mind, I had never forgotten those two men and the terrible things they had done. Deep down, I knew they were the reason boys made me so uncomfortable. My secret had weighed on my soul for so long that the idea of bearing it to the world was both frightening and a relief. "I'll go," I agreed in a small voice.

The following week, I sat across from a counselor, shifting uncomfortably in my seat. As the clock ticked away on the wall, I reluctantly shared my story. Tears spilled down my cheeks as I explained how two of my mother's friends, both whom I'd trusted, had molested me as a young girl. "They told me they would hurt my family if I told anyone," I added softly. Even now, eight years later, the pain was just as vivid, the words just as frightening.

"Your trust and your body were violated," the counselor said, validating my story. "It makes sense that you wouldn't want anything to do with boys, as they represent those two men you couldn't trust."

I nodded through my tears. The pieces of the puzzle were all coming together now. At last, I was free to shed the hurt I'd stuffed inside. I attended counseling sessions for the next couple of months, processing my abuse. But I still had yet to discover the secret to true healing in my heart.

When high school rolled around, I drifted away from youth group and took an interest in the party scene. It seemed everyone who was anyone partied on the weekends. In a small town with just a few burger joints on the corner, the teenagers soon grew restless, and the alcohol emerged. I enjoyed the freedom my parents allowed me and was happy to finally be part of the popular crowd.

I was no longer afraid to talk to boys and, in fact, had taken quite a liking to them. When I was 16, I met a guy who liked to party as well, and we soon became inseparable. After dating for about a year, I noticed that my period was overdue, but a pregnancy test turned up negative. One night, I lay curled in pain, crying, in my parents' bed. "Mom, I think I might be pregnant," I confided. Mom assured me she would stand beside me no matter what.

The next day, I began to bleed heavily, and Mom rushed me to the emergency room. A doctor confirmed that I had suffered a miscarriage. An ultrasound was done to see if I needed a dilation and curettage procedure to remove tissue and stop the bleeding.

As he waved the wand over my stomach, his brow furrowed. "Hmm. It looks like you're still pregnant. You must have been carrying twins."

"Twins?" I croaked.

"You still have a baby inside of you, but because of the way you've miscarried the first one, you'll most likely miscarry the second," he explained flatly.

My heart raced at the news. At just 16 years old, I had gotten pregnant with twins. Though deep down I knew I was too young, my heart broke for the children I would never see.

A few days later, I miscarried the second baby. My boyfriend and I broke up shortly after, and I tried to resume life, partying again on the weekends to forget my pain. After high school graduation, my parents and grandmother took me to Alaska to visit a friend of my mother. I was excited about the change of scenery.

"I know this nice boy down the street you should meet," my mother's friend said when we arrived. "I'll introduce you to him tonight."

That evening, a boy named Ben showed up on her doorstep to take me out. We decided to hang out at his friend's house and get to know each other. After about an hour of awkward conversation, he asked, "Want to go for a ride on a four-wheeler?"

"Sure," I said, eager for the adventure.

I climbed on the back of the four-wheeler, wrapped my arms tight around his waist and we headed for the trail. Up and over, up and over — we zoomed over hills at full throttle. Wind blowing across my face, I leaned into his back. Then, just as we rose over another hill, I saw the car. It was headed straight for us! I felt a quick hesitation of the bike's motor as my date tried to stop it on a dime. Both of us were thrown from the four-wheeler. As my body sailed toward the car's windshield, I caught the terrified look of two men in the car. I flipped through the air watching a dizzying spin of sky, ground, sky, windshield, sky — street!

The next few moments were a blur as I tried to stand up, shaken, scraped up and sore. My neck hurt terribly, and I could barely move. "What happened?" I mumbled, brushing the gravel off my tattered clothes.

Ben slowly stood to his feet. "Oh, man, you okay, Vykki? I'm so sorry!"

An hour later, I lay in the emergency room at the local hospital, a doctor hovering over me. "You got banged up pretty good there," he mused as he took my vitals. "Looks like you're going to wind up with a serious case of whiplash but nothing else too serious." I left the hospital in a neck brace.

Ben called a few days later, but I was too upset with him to call back. He persisted, and when I didn't return his several phone calls, a beautiful bouquet of flowers showed up on my doorstep. I finally gave in and took his next phone call. "Thank you for the flowers," I said. "I guess you're forgiven."

"It was an accident! I feel terrible!" Ben cried. "And you wouldn't return my calls. I didn't even know if you were okay!"

"I'm fine," I confirmed as I sniffed the bouquet beside me.

Ben and I went on a few more dates before I returned

to California. We talked a lot and realized how much we had in common. A few weeks later, he surprised me by moving to California. "I know I'm only 18, but I'm ready to do what I want," he told me. "And what I want is to be with you and try to make things work. I like you a lot, Vykki."

"I like you, too, Ben," I admitted. My family moved to another nearby desert town, and Ben and I began dating more seriously. But, like me, Ben eventually grew restless with the small-town life. We started fighting, and he decided to move back to Alaska. "I think it's for the best," I told him with a sad sigh.

Shortly after Ben left California, I sat in the bathroom with a little white stick, my hands shaking as I stared at the two pink lines. Ben was gone, and I was carrying his baby. I took a deep breath and made the dreaded call. "I'm pregnant," I told him bravely.

"Oh, Vykki, wow! What are you gonna do? Do you want me to move back down there? Or maybe you should move here, or maybe …"

"Ben, when you were here, we fought all the time," I reminded him. "I know being a single mother at 20 years old won't be easy, but I'd rather give this a go on my own than drag you into it and wind up miserable. What sort of example will that set for our child?"

Ben was quiet for a moment. At last, he spoke. "If that's what you want, Vykki. I don't know what else to say."

"There's not much to say. I'll be okay." As I hung up,

tears spilled down my cheeks. I knew Ben wasn't the right man for me, but the idea of parenting a child on my own was daunting. Still, I'd never had any question about keeping the baby. I would raise it alone. The next step was to break the news to my parents.

"Pregnant? Oh, wow, Vykki!" My father wiped tears from his eyes. He leaned in and took both my hands in his. "Honey, we love you and support you no matter what."

"Yes, we do," my mother chimed in, kissing my head. "We're here for you, sweetie."

"Thank you," I cried. "I'm going to be okay. I'm actually a little bit excited."

"Another grandchild! I'm going to be a grandmother again!" my mother exclaimed, laughing. "Wow, can you believe that!" At the time, my sister had five children, and my brother had one. This was grandchild number seven!

I was relieved to have my parents' support. My life was about to change in a major way, but somehow, I just knew we were all going to be okay.

As my belly expanded over the next several months, I grew excited about the little being inside of me. When my daughter, Savannah, came into the world, I marveled over her every delicate feature, unable to believe she was really mine. I had never seen anything so beautiful in all my life. "Look at all that hair," I murmured, nuzzling my nose in her soft head. I was young and alone, but I was certain of one thing: I was born to be this little girl's mother.

As Savannah grew from a tiny infant to a rosy-cheeked baby, I cherished every minute with her. One day, my sister called me, giggling. "Okay, what's this letter I got from you, signed Savannah's mommy? You're still Vykki, you know," she teased.

I laughed. "I know, I know." Savannah was my whole world, though. She clung to my side when we went out in public, her thick blond curls rubbing against my cheeks when friends stopped to greet her.

"What a beautiful little girl!" they gushed. "So much personality!"

When my friend suggested I meet her brother one day, I declined politely. "I don't think I need anyone else right now," I said. I was perfectly content being a single mother.

"He's really a great guy," she insisted. "Just come over and meet him. I promise, you won't regret it!"

I sighed. "All right. But he has to know something upfront. My daughter comes first."

When I met Joe, a staggering 6 feet, 7 inch, dark-haired handsome guy, my heart reconsidered. We laughed over dinner, and I told him about my beautiful daughter. "She's 9 months old and just the cutest thing you've ever seen," I gushed.

"Do you have any pictures?" Joe asked, showing genuine interest.

I whipped a photo out of my purse and slid it across the table. "She really is beautiful," he admitted. "She looks a lot like you."

I blushed at his words. I was falling for this guy I'd barely met, just after saying I was perfectly content as a single mother. What had gotten into me?

Home Is Where the Heart Is

Joe and I fell into a whirlwind romance. I loved the way he scooped Savannah in his arms and twirled her around, just as if she were his own. When he proposed just a few months after we'd begun dating, I happily accepted. We married six months after our first date and plunged into life as newlyweds — with a baby.

Joe and I purchased our first home together. I was elated to be a real family, and we soon talked of adding to our brood. When Savannah was 2 years old, I gave birth to another beautiful daughter, Sarah. Two years later, our son, Little Joe, came along. We decided our family was complete, and I threw myself into my role as a mother and wife. Life was good, it seemed, and I was content. Or so I thought.

One day, my husband called me into the other room with some devastating news. My beloved nephew, Brandon, just 16 years old, had passed away after drinking at a party. I fell to the floor in sobs, unable to believe he was gone. Brandon was my sister's child. The silly nickname, Peaches and Cream, had stuck, but as he grew older, I shortened it to Peaches so as not to embarrass him. We had shared many good laughs and special times, and I had been looking forward to his visit in just two days. Now, he was gone, leaving behind a gaping hole in my heart.

I sank into a deep depression after his death, crying for hours every day. I wandered around the house, going through the motions of life like a robot. Brandon's death ignited a new fear in me. *What if my husband or parents or children passed away, too? How would I cope if I lost someone else I loved?*

"Honey, I know this is so, so hard for you, but I'm here for you," Joe assured me one day when he found me sobbing on the bed. "Every day is going to get a little bit easier, I promise."

I was thankful for my husband's gentle support, but remembering the good times with my nephew only made me cry more. I wished we'd had just one last visit together, one more night to stay up late watching movies and laughing. While my sister remained in shock, my grief grew very real, stretching into parts of my heart I didn't know could hurt so much. My fear of losing someone else escalated, and the days became long, dreary and meaningless.

I would lay awake at night, pondering how I could take care of everyone, including my aging father and my bedridden mother. The stress pressed in on me night after night, and I cried myself to sleep. By day, I plastered a fake smile on my face and went through the motions of day-to-day life. I confided in Joe. We had a strong marriage, healthy and well-behaved children. We owned a nice home, and Joe had his own business. I was close to my parents, extended family and friends. I couldn't want for more. Still, I felt like something significant was missing. Was there something else? Or was I just ungrateful?

Home Is Where the Heart Is

One Sunday morning, I drove by a local church and watched as several families filed out the doors. They looked happy as they mingled with their friends, the children playing happily at their side. I hadn't set foot in church in years. In our small town, I thought those who attended church looked down on those who did not. I wondered what it might be like to walk through those doors again. Would God be angry that I hadn't showed up in a while? Would he remember all the rules I'd broken over my lifetime?

I focused on my family, trying to be the best mother I could. Savannah, Sarah and Little Joe were all growing up to be wonderful individuals, and I enjoyed every minute with them. I also grew closer to my parents, who were both ailing in their older age. But the lingering sadness remained, as well as a feeling that something was missing in our lives. "I just really feel like our lives aren't complete," I told Joe one night as we headed to bed.

"What do you mean?" he asked, his eyes wide. The last time he heard this, we ended up with our third child.

"I just feel like my life is a puzzle, and there is a huge piece missing," I mused. "I've searched everywhere for it and haven't found it. Maybe it's God that we're missing. I want to start taking the kids to church." Joe agreed.

We tried out a small church the following week, but it wasn't the right fit. Something still tugged at my heart, though, an indescribable desire to suddenly know more about God. I had experienced only bits and pieces of him over the years, but I'd never been able to put the whole puzzle together. My nephew's death had triggered not only a lingering sadness in my heart, but a deeper longing for more meaning.

After trying a few more small churches that didn't feel right, I grew restless. I had spent nearly my whole life in small towns. Perhaps what we needed was a change. A big change.

"Moving?" Joe asked when I shared my feelings with him. "Really, Vykki?"

"But wouldn't it be great to live in a beautiful, family-oriented place with great schools and low crime?" I said. "A place where maybe my parents could get better health care?" My mother's diabetes had worsened over the past several years, leaving her bedridden, and I was concerned with the care she received at her local doctor's office. Our life in Southern California was starting to feel stagnant. With the kids growing older, I was afraid they would experience the same small-town boredom I had as a teen and seek out trouble. The more I thought about it, the more I became convinced that a move would be best for us all.

A few years earlier, I had described to a friend the idyllic place I dreamed of to raise my children. She told me about Gig Harbor, Washington. Remembering her suggestion, I now researched the town. I learned that it's a small coastal town in Northern Washington. As I viewed photos on the Internet, its picturesque beauty took my breath away. Gig Harbor did, indeed, seem to embody everything I longed for. But I was a realist and a pessimist at that. How on earth would we ever get from a little town in Southern California all the way up to Washington?

"How would *that* ever happen, that you could move there?" people around me questioned. But Gig Harbor became my obsession, and I talked about it every day. The weather, the hospital being built, the toll bridge — people grew tired of my one-track mind. "You're a California girl," they would say. "You can't handle the rain. Quit being negative about your life here." But I kept searching for that puzzle piece to make my life complete.

Feeling somewhat lost when it came to God and church, I decided to pick up a children's Bible and start reading to my kids. I still wasn't sure of much, but I knew that I wanted my kids to grow up having a relationship with God. As I pored over the pages, I wondered if that far away, somewhat scary figure in the sky could really be the loving God my old youth pastor once described. And if so, how could I teach my kids about him when I hardly knew him myself?

One night, as I climbed into bed, I decided to ask God for his help. "God, please help me help my children get to know you better," I prayed. I wasn't sure if God was listening, especially to someone who hadn't talked to him much over the years, but I figured it was worth asking.

Just a few weeks later, the economy hit a record low point. Until then, Joe was reluctant about Gig Harbor. He thought it was just another of my attempts to fix my life. Now, gravely concerned about the growing economic crisis, he agreed to check out Gig Harbor. Our brother-in-law agreed to take a job-hunting trip to the coastal town. "If it's meant to be," they said, "we'll find work within a week." If not, they will have had a well-deserved vacation.

Again, I prayed as I lay in bed. "God, please be with them as they visit Washington. If we are meant to move to Gig Harbor, please let them find work and a home."

The very next day, my husband called with astounding news. "I just got offered a job!" he said excitedly.

"You're kidding!" I could hardly believe my ears. I'd grown a bit discouraged when I learned that the job market in Northern Washington was just as tough as it was in Southern California. The fact that God had given him a job in our dream place was nothing short of a miracle. "Wow, I can't believe it! We're moving!" I cried, ecstatic.

The next day, the excitement continued.

"Did I mention I found us a house, too?" Joe added. The men had found a house with a short-term lease that could accommodate both our families while we searched for homes of our own.

"Wow," I repeated. This was all happening so fast. My heart's desire was finally fulfilled. God had heard my prayer and answered it!

The men returned home, and we packed our things into a moving truck on a sunny December morning for the long drive up to Washington. The California blue skies faded into the distance, replaced by dark, damp skies as we crossed the state border. But despite the dismal weather, I remained cheery and excited. God and I were still new acquaintances, but I was confident he was 100 percent behind our move.

As we entered Gig Harbor and the stunning waterfront properties came into view, I held my breath, nearly pinching myself as my dream became a reality. We were finally home.

The first thing I wanted to do after we unpacked our necessities was find a good church. That Sunday, we tried out a large church we had found online. The people were friendly enough, but the experience was overwhelming. "I think a smaller church is more our speed," Joe said.

The following week, we stepped into a small church, Harbor Life. I felt completely at ease as several families stopped to greet us. As the pastor spoke, he stopped and glanced around the room. "I feel like there is a couple here who is seeking to reconcile with God. You used to know him, but you have drifted away and are wanting to rebuild your relationship with him."

My heart pounded so loudly I wondered if anyone might hear it. I knew without a doubt that he was talking about us. The pastor asked who this might be. I watched Joe raise his hand, and slowly, I raised my hand, too, tears filling my eyes. The pastor smiled warmly and nodded. "Lord, we just ask you to draw this young couple back to you," he prayed. "They are here because they want to know you more deeply. Would you please remind them how much you love them, that you have never left their side?"

After the service, we went up to shake the pastor's hand. "Thank you so much for praying for us. You have no idea how much that meant," Joe told him gratefully. "We will definitely be back."

I could hardly wait to discuss the service with Joe when we got in the car. "Wasn't that amazing?" I gushed as we headed home. "I can't believe the pastor was talking right to us! I really feel like this is where we're supposed to be. I think God brought us to Gig Harbor to find Harbor Life."

While dismal skies often ignite depression, my new surroundings did the opposite for me. I was suddenly filled with a fresh, optimistic attitude about life. I realized I had spent most of my life under a pessimistic cloud, often fearing the worst. I'd tried so hard to control everything, to fix not only my own problems, but my parents' as well. Was it possible God was really working in the little details of our life? Did he really care that much?

After we settled into our new home, I encouraged my parents to join us in Gig Harbor. "I would love it if you moved up here," I invited. "It would be nice to be close so I could help you out." They put their house on the market.

One day, I called to see how their open house went. "This is a tough housing market," my father admitted. "But we'll see what happens."

I had been praying more and had now learned to rely on God for everything. I was convinced he would answer my prayer for my parents to join us in Gig Harbor.

Home Is Where the Heart Is

In a few weeks, my mother called with astounding news. "We sold the house!" she announced. "Can you believe it? Just like that, we got a buyer!"

I clutched the phone in shock. "You're kidding! Mom, that's amazing!" These days, I couldn't stop pinching myself. Things were falling into place all too perfectly. "You're going to love it up here!" I told her excitedly.

"Thank you, Lord," I cried when I got off the phone. "I truly see you working here." My mother's health had worsened in the last year, so I could not wait to get her the help she needed upon their move.

After my parents arrived, I took them to the local doctor for checkups. My father needed a new pacemaker, and the doctor assured us he could do the procedure as soon as possible. But for my mother, he had grim news. "We ran some tests, and it looks like you have breast cancer," he told her.

Cancer? My heart skipped a beat as he went on, describing the diagnosis and the treatment plan. Despite the solemn situation, I felt an indescribable peace inside. A year before, this sort of news would have sent me over the edge, but as I attended Harbor Life and learned to trust in God more, I realized our lives were truly in his hands. I could make a choice right now to be filled with fear and fall apart, or I could choose to give my mother over to God and believe that he would work it all for good.

"I know God will cure you, Mom," I told my mother with confidence as we drove home that afternoon. "Everything is going to be just fine."

"Thank you, sweetie." My mother took my hand and squeezed it. "I sure hope so," she added softly.

Joe, the children and I prayed each night for my mother as her surgery neared. God's presence continued to flood my heart with peace, and once again, I reminded myself that he was in control of the ultimate outcome for our lives.

On the day of my mother's double mastectomy, I accompanied her to the hospital. As the doctors prepped her, they tried to pry off a treasured ring — her father's wedding ring. She had worn it for so long that it was practically embedded in her finger. "We can't operate with that thing on," they explained. But the ring wouldn't budge.

"We'll have to cut it off," the doctor concluded after several attempts. "I'm sorry."

My mother glanced over at me, her eyes sad. I knew how much that ring meant to her; cutting it off would be devastating. "Can I try to remove it?" I asked.

"No harm in trying," she said, shrugging.

As I applied liquid soap, Mom said the nurse had already tried that. It didn't work for me, either.

God, I prayed as I tugged at the ring, *please help me get this off her finger. It means so much to her.* Suddenly, the ring loosened. "It's coming! It's coming!" Mom exclaimed as it slid over her knuckle and into my hand.

I held it up as a trophy. "God took this off! He wants you to know he's here with you, Mama!" I assured her. I had no doubt that God would watch over her in that operating room.

The surgery was successful, and not long after that day, we all received the good news we'd been praying for: My mother's cancer was cured! "Thank you, Lord, for curing my mother. You are so good!" I praised him again. These days, I couldn't stop thanking God for his goodness. We truly had so much to be thankful for.

My children got involved at Harbor Life Church, and I loved watching them grow as they learned more about God. I thought of my church days as a child and how fearful and confused I'd felt when it came to God and his so-called rules. Somewhere between the kneeling and the sitting and reading the verses, I'd missed the simple truth of the Bible: God is love. He loved me so much he'd sent his son, Jesus, to die on the cross in my place for the wrong things I'd done. He wasn't a big guy in the sky, ready to smite me if I messed up, but rather, he wanted a relationship with me. He knew life would be hard, but his promises were true, and if I believed them, I could experience a peace that only came from him. At last, I had found that indescribable peace, and I was grateful my family had, too.

As I read my Bible before bed one night, I stumbled onto Matthew 7:7 and read these words: "Ask and it will be given to you; seek and you will find; knock and the door will be opened to you." I realized once again just how powerful prayer was. God *wanted* us to come to him with our heart's desires; he simply wanted us to ask. He had opened that door for us, and it was here that my heart had truly been healed.

"Mom, wait up!" My mother sprinted ahead of me as we strolled down to the coffee shop one morning. It was a beautiful, rare sunny day in Gig Harbor, the thick pine trees a perfect backdrop to the still blue waters on the horizon. Since her surgery, my mother had become a new woman. Her diabetes was under control, she had lost a significant amount of weight and now had the energy of a teenager. In fact, some days, I could hardly keep up with her.

My mother laughed as she slowed down to catch her breath. "Hurry up, slow poke," she teased.

As my tennis shoes pounded the pavement, I couldn't help but be giddy. I had so much to be thankful for: a beautiful home, a healthy family, a church we loved and a new outlook on life. My sad, lonely days were behind me. I no longer tried to control things, but instead turned them over to God. His plan and his timing, I'd learned, were far better than mine. And in that perfect timing, he'd given me the desire of my heart and led us to Gig Harbor. I was finally home, but more than that, I'd found the missing puzzle piece to fill the void in my heart. I'd found a trusting relationship with God.

An Orphan's Journey

The Story of Bill Lash

Written by Karen Russell Holmes

I looked out the window as I rode the Greyhound bus with my mother, older brother, Dennis, and baby brother, Ronald. At 3 years old, our destination did not matter to me because this was fun. The bus whizzed down the highway, gently bouncing me in my seat until we arrived in Northern Seattle. Our adventure continued with a taxi ride. Wow, what a treat!

The taxi stopped in front of a large brick four-story building. My mother paid the taxi driver, and we walked inside. Dennis and I were ushered into a large room filled with playing boys of all sizes and ages. I thought I hit the jackpot for a good time. It seemed we were going on a campout!

"Let's go play with the other kids," Dennis encouraged.

"Alright," I agreed since he was older and seemed to be okay with it.

On that day in 1954, I watched people through a window take my baby brother from my mother's arms, scrub him clean from top to bottom and put new clothes on him.

That was the last time I saw Ronald or my mother. We weren't camping out.

This was a state orphanage.

Changing Course

I don't remember my dad because I was so little when he deserted our family. My mother soon started dating another man.

One day he told her, "It's me or your boys." She chose him.

At 3, everyone but Dennis had either abandoned me or was taken from me, but somehow I felt secure — even loved.

We were not at the orphanage for long when my Uncle Willis and Aunt Esther came from California and rescued us. They had learned of our misfortune, and their friends Tex and Mildred wanted to raise us because they couldn't have children of their own. Unable to conceive, the couple loved us as though we'd been their children all along.

A few months later, Dennis began to tease me as we played catch in the yard. "Na-na, you can't get it," he chided, hugging the ball and glove tight as he turned away.

"Give it back!" I demanded, trying to pry his arms away from his chest.

Just then, our new parents called us inside. I rushed into the house, eager to retaliate by tattling about something Dennis did earlier in the day.

"Dennis poked holes in the backseat of the car with his pocketknife," I squealed rushing breathless into the house.

Tex and Mildred did not seem to be listening. "You have to go back to the orphanage," Tex said.

It's my fault for tattling, I thought.

A state official had just phoned them to say that my aunt and uncle never had the legal right to take us out of the orphanage. "Those children are wards of the state," he said. "You must bring them back immediately."

Even after returning us to the orphanage, the couple fought hard to adopt us. Ultimately, they were refused because they had been separated at one time. They later had children of their own.

Life at the orphanage wasn't all bad because, aside from those months with Tex and Mildred, I didn't know any other life. Every weekend we went on outings up to the falls or to a park. I slept with all the other boys in one big room lined with cot-like beds while our housefather slept in his own room.

Out of the 43 boys at the orphanage, I was the youngest. This made me the whipping boy. I was picked on, but again I did not know there was a better life.

"You're just a scrawny little runt," an older boy taunted in the hallway. "I'll bet your belt can't even hold up your pants," he mocked and proceeded to pull my pants down.

I'll get you somehow, someway, I thought.

I did find a way to retaliate. In the cafeteria during dinner, I threw juice on him and ran and hid. I did not let them get away with bothering me. We did not have much of anything we could call our own. If I was holding something an older or larger boy wanted, then that possession soon became his. I always found a way to put them in their place, though.

At the orphanage we didn't hold much of anything sacred. We didn't celebrate birthdays or holidays — not even Easter or Christmas. They did not take us to the little church across the street, but somehow I got there — I don't remember who took me. I made deals with God ("if you do this for me, I'll do that for you"). But one day, when I was about 6 or 7, I learned Elvis was King.

On that day, several black Cadillacs pulled up to the curb outside our building. The girls screamed uncontrollably, clapping and jumping as men in suits got out of the cars. Elvis Presley was here at our orphanage! He came to visit while in town for the World's Fair.

Dennis did not make out so well at the orphanage. He took everything to heart, and I was more happy-go-lucky. Due to his personality and because he was older, Dennis understood a little bit better what happened to us and had a harder time with our abandonment. His life at the orphanage was short lived, because he became a troublemaker. When I was with him, I would be disciplined, too.

One time the counselor was going to spank us for something we did. I put a book in my pants so I would not feel the swats. I pretended that the spanking hurt and cried and carried on. The next time, Dennis used my idea and put a whole bunch of books in his pants. Since the books were so noticeable, he was caught, and of course this ruined my chances to continue to use my little scheme.

"That was stupid, Dennis," I said under my breath. "Now I won't be able to do that again." After that the counselor made us lower our pants and spanked our bare bottoms.

Dennis continued to rebel so much that he was sent to reform school. One more person had left me. By the age of 6, my mother had abandoned me, my brothers had been taken from me and I'd been yanked out of a loving home. Still, somehow, I felt secure.

Soon, I joined the rank and file of children walking to and from the neighborhood public school from the orphanage. I liked school because I was no longer the smallest or youngest. Being in a class of kids my age and size gave me an advantage I never experienced. I had learned well what being older and bigger meant. I saw the chance to take what I wanted and became the bully.

When I was 8, a couple named the Lashes contacted the orphanage to adopt a child. They had been unable to have children, and the administrator of the orphanage decided that out of all the boys, I needed a home the most. I was not interested in leaving the orphanage (I was happy there), so they made me stay with the Lashes for a trial period of a week. I was to decide if I wanted them, and they were to decide if they wanted me. At the orphanage I would watch the older boys ride bikes, and I really wanted one. The Lashes had a bike, and I was allowed to ride it whenever I wanted, so I agreed to be their son. Adoptions cost $350 at the time, and the Lashes were unable to afford me. However, the orphan society authorities decided to give me to the Lashes for free.

Mom and Dad Lash lived in a town south of Seattle and, like at the orphanage, I walked to school. However, at the school I had been attending, educating the orphans was not priority. The teachers did not require the orphans to do schoolwork, so we just slid by. I thought my friend who lived down the street was a genius because he could read highway signs. I could not even tell time.

"Bill, could you please read the next paragraph?" my teacher asked on my second day of school.

"Th-th-theee … rrrrr-e-p," I stammered as I tried to sound out the words in my social studies book. All I had retained were the sounds of letters.

"Bill, would you mind letting Laura read next? We'll talk after class."

Relieved that I did not have to go on, I nodded my head, and Laura took up where I left off. She sounded to me like she had been reading for 50 years.

"I don't think you have learned to read," my teacher kindly said, working hard not to hurt my feelings. "We're going to have to put in some extra time after school together so you can learn how to read as well as the other children. Would you like that?"

"Yes, ma'am," I stammered, actually relieved that she thought I wasn't too dumb to learn.

Third grade literally became my first grade. My adoptive parents sent me to take an aptitude test, and the results came back placing me above average, but I would just do enough to get by. I caught up to my grade level in that year, but the "just enough to get by" summed up the rest of my school years.

Mom Lash was a tiny 90-pound spitfire. She put a lot of time, energy and prayers into this little boy so he might make something of himself. Dad Lash was fine at first, but he'd had my mom to himself for many years and was now having trouble sharing her attention with me. We butted heads quite often, and he was jealous of me from time to time. He was a good man, but he was hard.

One time, when I was 10, he was in the garage working on the car. I saw that he was in danger of hurting himself while he strained to turn a stubborn bolt.

"You better not do that. You're going to get hurt," I warned, and sure enough the wrench slipped, and he hit his hand.

In anger he threw the wrench across the garage, hitting the wall.

He looked at me and growled, "I hate you."

I looked back at him and retorted, "Well, Dad, the feeling is mutual."

I knew he did not mean it, and what I said to him hurt him 10 times worse than he was trying to hurt me, but we simply did not get along. The friction in our relationship kept me from opening my heart to loving more than one person at a time, so I connected with Mom.

Unfortunately, my mother was caught between the two of us. She did the best she could to appease both of us and felt bad about our problems.

Dad wasn't all to blame. I was ornery, too. I was disrespectful, often mouthing off to my mother. I did things like shoot out the neighbor's window with my BB gun and managed to keep it to myself. However, when the neighbor is the sheriff, he has a way of finding out who did it. Dad confronted me about the broken window when the sheriff told him what I had done.

"Did you shoot out the neighbor's window?" he asked, glaring at me.

"No, I did not," I lied.

He didn't believe me. "I'll just take you back to that orphanage and trade you in for a girl is what I'll do!" he threatened, though he didn't follow through.

Even through those tough times, I still felt that underlying perception of being secure and loved.

One bright spot in my teenage years was Brenda. I met Brenda at church during my eighth grade year. Mom and Dad were Christians and attended a Four Square Church. Brenda actually lived and went to school in the next town over, but we attended the same church.

"That's the girl I'm going to marry," I said to my buddy when I laid eyes on her.

Brenda and I became friends and started dating in high school, even though we went to different schools. At the end of my sophomore year, I wanted to go to school with her.

When school started my junior year, I asked my principal if I could transfer to Brenda's school.

"I'll grant you a transfer as long as you stay out of trouble," the principal said.

"I can do that! Thanks," I said with a grin on my face. But my promise was not easily kept.

"I'm an example of a real man," the teacher spouted off in class one day strutting around at the front of the room.

We'll see about that, I thought to myself and set out to find a way to prove him wrong.

While eating lunch in the cafeteria, I saw my chance. As the teacher passed by my table with his tray full of food, I shoved off in my chair to knock him down. Not the most coordinated effort on my part. I ended up putting my head through the wall and missing him completely. When a buddy of mine started to take the rap for me, I confessed. Instead of good behavior being my ticket to switch schools, the principal decided to let me go just to get rid of me. The transfer was granted.

My troubled relationship with my dad often boiled over into outbursts from me. I worked at the church for a while, cleaning, and I remember going down to the basement where no one could hear me and screaming cuss words and punching my fists into the concrete walls.

The pastor at the time became concerned. No one knew that side of me. He came into the church one time when I was cleaning the chapel. I was mad about something. I ranted and raved curses into the air with such anger, I scared the poor man badly.

Something was coming, though, that was about to change my whole life a little at a time. Our church youth group was preparing to go to camp, and since Brenda was going, you bet I was going to be there, too. One night the preacher was saying that God wanted to be my friend and wanted me to live forever with him in heaven. However, the preacher said I didn't deserve to experience that because of the wrong things I'd done in life, no matter how big or small. God made a way, though, by sending his son, Jesus, to take the rap for my faults by being killed on a cross. Now, all I had to do was ask God's forgiveness and be thankful to Jesus, and I could be God's friend. *Jesus, God's son, did that for me?* I was impressed.

I went back to my cabin and talked to God about what the man had said. My prayer was like seeing and talking to God through a straw. I could see him, but he could not hear me, and he would not look at me. My prayers up until then had been nothing more than deal-making with God. I did not know that I could really know God in an intimate friendship. When I did not seem to be getting through to God, I became scared, thinking I had committed some unforgivable sin that kept me from being close to God.

I reported this to one of the counselors.

"Hey, everyone, come with me," he said, gathering all the counselors to the lunchroom. "Bill needs our help."

Circling in close around me, they began praying for me. As they spoke, I began to understand what a relationship with God meant for the first time. As these counselors talked out loud to God about me, I felt all my anger and rage melting away. From that point forward, my friendship with God slowly started to grow. Was God the reason for my feelings of security and love all those years? Where the feeling came from, I don't know, but somehow I finally made the connection with God's love.

Eventually, though, the friction between my dad and I drove me to make a desperate decision. When I was 16, my parents had gone on a month-long vacation, and I stayed home. During their trip I stole my dad's car and burned up the transmission. I also used the lawnmower without permission to mow the yard of the people who kept me during my parents' trip. When my parents got home, the car did not work, and Dad knew who to blame, but I would not admit to the dirty deed.

"Did you do this?" my dad questioned angrily. "Taking someone's things without permission is stealing. Just for that I'm going to call the police and have you arrested."

"Don't worry. I'm not going to be here when they come," I told him, my mind spinning.

Our argument took place on the day the astronauts landed on the moon for the first time, and we had just finished Sunday dinner. I moved out and never went back. Amazingly, my dad and I became closer after that. (Sadly, after my mother passed away many years later, he ended up with dementia. His temperament changed, and he became a sweet old man.) Though I had moved out, I still had a relationship with my parents. I just did not live with them.

I took up residence with a Vietnam veteran and a member of our church named Dan. Dan made it through the war in more than one tour without a scratch, but lost an arm to a gunshot wound given to him by his brother-in-law over a card game. I lived with him for about six months, until I was able to afford my own apartment.

Though I'm sure people at the church and others reached out to me, I was like Fonzie in *Happy Days* doing my own thing and unable to take gifts. I even wore a white t-shirt and a jacket with jeans all the time and a pair of pointy shoes. I was the type of person who would rather give than receive.

I also worked at a restaurant starting as a dishwasher and climbing up to a dinner cook. I was in the money, I thought, making $25 a week as a dishwasher! With that money I could afford to live on my own, all the while going to school. I was feeling pretty good about my situation until my senior year when the restaurant burned down. All of a sudden, I was out of a job. For the first time in my life, I felt insecure. Through abandonment by my mother, losing my brothers, living in an orphanage and the trouble with my father, I had never had an insecure moment that I remembered, until now.

Moving out had a way of making me grow up quickly. I knew I could not get into trouble or I would be sent home. However, there were times when I goofed around drinking and raising Cain with my friends.

"Drop me off here," I told the driver on one of those carousing nights. "I need to call my girlfriend."

"Oh, he has to call his ball and chain," the guys teased.

The driver stopped the car by a payphone and drove off. Minutes later, they were arrested. Being rescued without even knowing it was now happening to me all the time. Someone was protecting me, that same protection and feeling of love I had known in the back of my mind all my life. However, living alone left me without that one person to love. Brenda took up that position, and my focus was now on her. She had been one of the only steady relationships in my life, and why she stuck with me, I don't know — probably that protection again.

Graduation rolled around, and my mother beamed with pride as I walked across the stage to receive my diploma. Brenda was still in high school, but I knew she was the one for me.

After high school in March of 1971, I joined the Air Force at 19. I knew I was going to get drafted, so I decided to go ahead and join. My draft card was mailed to me at boot camp! Because the Vietnam War had not ended, I thought I was a goner. However, I ended up being stationed stateside. In that first year, I finally made the connection between the protection I was receiving and God. My roommate was a big doper, and one night he and a bunch of us were all sitting around a campfire.

"Hey, try this out, man" he said, handing me what looked like a hand-rolled cigarette.

I didn't know what it was, so I smoked it.

"How'd it make you feel?" my roommate wondered.

"All it did was give me a headache."

"Then you need to try this stuff," he pushed and gave me an opium-soaked joint.

I smoked that, and I thought the top of my head was going to pop off. After that, I never touched any of the stuff again. *Why would anyone want to feel like that?* I thought, but I realized that the bad experience was God's way of protecting me. I finally put two and two together. He protected me.

Because of the pot-smoking experience and attending a good church in Colorado Springs, it was in the Air Force that I finally gave myself completely over to living the way God liked me to live. I set some goals, and God granted me those goals. When the goals were met at age 23, I thought, *Am I going to die now?* But God pointed out that I just needed to set new goals. A pattern for my life had been set, though, and I knew God was the one who had orchestrated my life all along. He was that underlying love and security I felt from the beginning.

As soon as Brenda graduated from high school, we were married. I had my one person to love, and life was good. I trained to be an electrician and loved my work in the Air Force.

God had been teaching me many things, but loving more than one person was a concept I still could not wrap my mind around. I saw the loving way Brenda interacted with her parents and siblings, but for the life of me, I could not figure out how she loved all of them and me, too. It did not make much sense to me.

Then, Tyson, our first of three children, was born.

When I held that tiny, helpless baby for the first time, smelling his hair and hearing the coos he made, I looked at Brenda and exclaimed, "I get it!"

Joy rushed over me, and I finally understood how a person's heart could be big enough to love more than one person at a time. Mine was bursting with love for Tyson and Brenda. I loved two people!

"God did this, didn't he?" I questioned my wife, smiling until my cheeks hurt.

"Yes," she said simply.

"I want to love *more* people!"

You will, I felt my heart say.

Never Alone

The Story of Shannon

Written by Alice McGhee

"See you guys later," I called to the other girls on my high school basketball team. We'd won our last game of the season, and as I zipped up my jacket and transferred my gym bag from one shoulder to the other, I couldn't help but replay the winning shot over and over again in my mind. It was a great way to end the first half of my freshman year. Tomorrow began Christmas break.

"See you in the New Year!" I hollered to my friends, who were equally as eager for two weeks of no alarm clocks and no homework.

Though Christmas was only days away, fall lingered in the air. As my mother and I walked to the car, my gym shoes crunched the remnants of fall that still lay in small piles scattered throughout the school parking lot, and I took a deep breath of the cool, but moderate, Washington air.

As I opened my car door, my mother's soft, warm eyes widened in fright. They were suddenly laser-focused on mine as if to convey a message her lips could not yet speak. A warning gasp escaped from her lips and …

Wham!

I was suddenly pressed between our car and the opposing team's 15-passenger school bus. My head and body were pinned.

Amazingly, I had no pain, but I labored to breathe as the pressure squeezed my lungs.

"You're killing my daughter! You need to move the bus!" Mom screamed as she and others tried in vain to push the bus off of me. Gears ground as the driver, in his panic, struggled to get the bus from reverse into first gear. Finally, he succeeded, releasing me from my metal vice.

Limp and unable to move, I felt my legs collapse beneath me and my body fall to the ground.

My parents had a rocky marriage, and it was the second marriage for both of them. Mom had one girl from her first marriage before her husband was killed in an auto accident. Dad had a couple of sons.

My dad struggled with alcohol abuse, which seemed to be a generational problem in his family. His happy-go-lucky drinking moods were often followed by stupors of self-pity. "I'm no good. I'm a lousy husband and father," he would whine. Then he would pass out.

Eventually, my mother had enough. She loved my father, and even after asking him to leave, she held out hope that he would change his ways. "You need help," she told him, over and over again.

Each time, he insisted, "I don't have a problem, so I don't need any help." After a number of years, Dad filed for divorce.

At first, Dad would come around every once in a

while. I was a daddy's girl, and his smile brightened my day. When he taught me to jitterbug, there were no arms as warm or strong as Dad's. I longed for his comforting embrace every day. When those arms released my body and those hands fell from my hair, I would sometimes follow them up his body to glassy eyes that occasionally swelled with tears. I didn't know if these moods were sincere or induced by alcohol, but I knew I felt loved, even if I did feel abandoned. I would often look out the window or front door and pretend I could see him coming to see me. But eventually, even those make-believe cars stopped pulling up in my driveway.

One summer when I was in elementary school, my mother took me to summer camp. She dropped me off with my suitcase and sleeping bag on the corner, just a few doors from the camp building.

I was terrified! What if she didn't come back to pick me up? My faithful mother had never given me a reason to think that she would abandon me. But, perhaps because my father had done so, I worried I'd be left to fend for myself.

Camp activities distracted me somewhat from my anxiety. Each day we played games, made crafts and had a chapel service. But things were a little different on the last night of the summer camp. The speaker read a Bible verse, Joshua 1:5: "I will never leave you, nor forsake you."

"This means that Jesus will always, always, always be with us," the man explained. "He will never leave us on our own to figure things out for ourselves. He loves us so much. If you want to have Jesus as part of your life and have him always with you, come down to the front and kneel as we pray together."

Someone who was guaranteed not to leave me alone? That sounded so good! I longed for someone who would never abandon me. I went to the front of the room and kneeled on the dusty orange shag carpeting. The speaker prayed with me to ask Jesus to be with me forever.

"Mom, I am so glad you are here!" I said the next day as she arrived to pick me up. "I was a little afraid you might not come. I really missed you, Mom!"

"You should know, Shannon, I would never leave you. I told you I would come back today to pick you up, didn't I? You're my daughter! I love you!"

After that week at camp, I practically inhaled the Bible. I just read it all the time, like I couldn't get enough of it. I was like a thirsty girl, and the Bible was my satisfying drink of water. If I did not have my Bible to read and study, I would have felt like God did not keep his promise to always be with me.

As I moved from elementary school to junior high, then from junior high to high school, I soaked up more of God's love for me. But as a busy basketball-playing teenager, I didn't think much about God's constant protection. Until that December night just before Christmas break.

"Talk to me, Shannon!" my mother shouted as she flew to the place where I had been wedged between her car and the school bus.

The coach of the opposing team that day had driven their basketball team to our school in the small school bus. The coach was having some difficulty backing up the bus. He eased up a small incline in reverse so that he could make the turn to get out of the parking lot.

"No, no, stop!" several people shouted as they pounded on the side of the bus.

The driver caught on to what was happening and pulled forward, releasing me from the crushing steel of the vehicles. I fell to the ground.

As I stared up at my mom from my place on the pavement, I felt … normal.

Standing to my feet, my eyes scanned my body that had been slowly crushed between several tons of metal just moments before.

"I think I am fine, Mom," I reassured her. "I don't hurt at all! I think Jesus saved me!" I exclaimed, jumping up and down wildly.

"I am sure he did, but we are headed for the hospital, anyway," Mom insisted, shaking her head with a relieved smile.

My enthusiastic display continued until my mother had to insist that I get in the car. "Shannon, I understand you are excited, but please, get in the car right now. We are headed for the hospital."

An X-ray showed I had no broken bones. A member of the hospital staff told me I was in "God's Zone" now. I couldn't stop telling everyone how wonderful God was for not abandoning me to be crushed. But as an extra precaution, the hospital staff wanted a surgeon to examine me the next morning. *There goes my first day to sleep in on Christmas vacation,* I thought.

The surgeon was puzzled that I still had no pain. "You need immediate surgery. There is a major break down the length of your jaw," he insisted. He looked me intently in the eye and said soberly, "You are a very lucky girl that your bones didn't crush your brain or that your head didn't pop off." I went home with his instructions to pack a bag, eat nothing and return that evening for surgery.

Even in the recovery room, I still had no pain. "It just doesn't seem possible," I told my mother.

"See, God is right there to hold your hand and be with you all the time," she reminded me.

My jaw was wired shut while it healed. No Christmas cookies for me! I had to eat everything through a straw. When my birthday came in January, I mixed my cake with lots and lots of ice cream until I could get it through a straw. I wasn't giving up pizza, either, so I tore it up into little pieces and mixed it with water to get it through my straw.

Never Alone

By the time I headed off to college, I was ready to look for whatever God wanted to do with my life. One semester, I took a part-time job as an intern children's pastor at a church. Part of my responsibility was accompanying a group of students ages 10 to 16 to Tijuana, Mexico. The goal of the trip was to help some missionaries in local neighborhoods and spend some time working in an orphanage there.

One day, we looked forward to some free time at the market for souvenir shopping followed by another orphanage visit. We would not have enough time to go to the market and then back to the place where we were staying to eat lunch before going to the orphanage. So we decided to make peanut butter and jelly sandwiches and take them with us.

"I think we will need about 50 sandwiches to feed our group, and what we have left over we can give to the children at the orphanage," I told another woman in our group.

"We have two loaves of bread and not very much peanut butter or jelly," she said.

As I looked into the jars I realized that there was only about one-fourth of a cup of peanut butter and one-fourth of a cup of jelly. I knew that would not be nearly enough for 50 sandwiches.

"Karen, let's just spread the peanut butter and jelly as thinly as we can and see how far it goes." We started making sandwiches, and I realized that Karen was spreading the peanut butter very thickly on the bread. So I asked her, "Don't you think we should spread the peanut butter thinner so we can make more sandwiches?"

"Oh, I am sorry, I was just spreading it like I usually do. We have made all of one loaf of bread into sandwiches and most of the second, and there seems to be plenty of peanut butter left."

I paused.

"There must be a mistake," I said, looking around for the barely filled jars I had seen when we first arrived. "Let me see the jar. I cannot imagine how that small amount of peanut butter made all these sandwiches and there is still more."

As I peered into each container, it looked as if we hadn't removed any peanut butter from the jar at all! I blinked and passed it off as a strange coincidence as one of the kids stacked the sandwiches in bread wrappers and prepped them for our hungry crowd. When we finished, there was peanut butter and jelly to spare.

We threw the bags of sandwiches into the back of the van. As we pulled up to the orphanage, one of the other adults began looking for the bags of sandwiches but only found one. "Keep looking. That other bag has to be here somewhere," I encouraged. But we had left it behind on the kitchen counter.

All 17 members of our group took one sandwich. But as I tallied the number of people in our group and the number of sandwiches we had put together, I realized that we hadn't even made that many. Everyone that wanted a second sandwich got one. The kids on our trip never even knew we were short. Somehow, what looked like barely enough had turned into more than enough with some left over.

It reminded me of a Bible story I knew. In 1 Kings 17:7-15, God told a man named Elijah to visit a widow and ask her for some food. When Elijah got there, he found the widow only had enough food for one last meal for her son and herself. In spite of this, she fed Elijah first and still had plenty of food left for her son and herself.

"I think our sandwiches were like the widow's food," I mused to several adults on the team. Our outwardly looking meager food supply had also been made into plenty.

At that moment, I felt we weren't alone. Someone was looking out for us, taking care of every need, big and small. My earthly father may have not been able to stay involved in my life, but I could not deny a heavenly father was leading me in every dance step along the way.

After college, I worked part time as a pastoral intern at a church for two years. I taught a group of energetic third-graders for a short time and then moved on to teach first grade in another city for 12 years. I currently teach preschool at a Christian school.

By the time I was 37, various friends had set me up on many blind dates. Even though I didn't feel the need for a man to complete me, I was willing to date. Then one day, my friend Nancy told me about Mark, from her church, Harbor Life. She didn't have to twist my arm to go to Harbor Life to meet Mark after a service. Ten years before, I had called that church home and still had many close friends there.

As we met in the lobby after the service, Nancy introduced Mark and me. "Mark, I would like for you to meet my friend Shannon. You guys get acquainted, and I'll talk to you later." Off she marched and left me standing there with Mark and his young son. We talked a little and scheduled a coffee date. From that point on we talked constantly. Since I was 37 and Mark was 39, we didn't want to waste each other's time. We had conversations you don't normally have that early in a relationship because we were serious about deciding if we were right for each other. I appreciated Mark's honesty as he poured out his heart to me. I felt I could trust him, and he would not hurt me or abandon me. Eventually, we decided to marry.

Even though my dad had drifted in and out of my life over the years, I loved him and wanted him to be part of my big day. "Hey, Dad," I said on the phone. "This is Shannon. I wanted to tell you that I am engaged to be married!"

He congratulated me.

"Dad, would you walk me down the aisle? It would really mean a lot to me," I invited.

Then I mustered my courage to say, "But if you are drunk, my brother will step in and take your place. It's important to me for you to have the honor, but I want you to do it sober."

"Yes, I can do that," he answered.

"And there's one other thing that would mean a lot to me," I continued. "Would you do the jitterbug with me as our father-bride dance?" I'm quite sure he beamed at the other end of the phone.

"Absolutely!" he exclaimed. My parents entered jitterbug competitions in my childhood and had taught me the playful dance. It was a special bond between my parents and me.

We had a traditional wedding ceremony at Harbor Life Church. The decorations and bridal party were beautiful in black and white. Red accents all around represented my mother, who had died six years earlier; it was her favorite color.

I held a bouquet of red roses and greens as I walked the aisle on my sober father's arm. I caught a glimpse of tears slipping down his cheeks. I felt closer to my dad on my wedding day than any other day in my life. He had come through for me that day. He had given up the drink for one magical day, just for me.

Our guests were given a silver box shaped like a pyramid. "I wonder what is inside?" they asked each other. "Why can't we open them?" A few people said, "I heard something scratching inside my box."

Finally, I announced, "All right. Everyone, open your boxes!" To everyone's delight a beautiful Painted Lady butterfly flew out of each box. They were so beautiful!

Normally the butterflies would have flown off into the sky, but a light breeze drifted in, keeping the butterflies from being comfortable to fly off. Instead, they rested on many people's heads and shoulders. It isn't every day a person gets sat on by a butterfly!

One of my favorite pictures is of Mark's and my index fingers touching end to end with a butterfly sitting on them. As we released our Painted Ladies, knowing they each came from a chrysalis where they were bound up and were now free, this symbolized new life to both Mark and me.

The magic continued at the reception. *Shuffle forward, shuffle back.* My father and I pranced around the dance floor to the upbeat music, one arm around each other's waists, my free hand clasped in his. *Twirl in, twirl out, shuffle forward, shuffle back.* We grinned and laughed. I savored every moment and every step. Guests teared up at the sight of my loving, sober father playfully swinging his daughter across the dance floor. I was daddy's girl again, if only for one song.

Several months after the wedding, Mark and I curled up on the sofa for some warm conversation as had become our habit. A fire burned in our gas fireplace, and candles flickered on the mantle. Mark's tender hands tucked my lap quilt snugly around my body, then held me close. I heard his heart's steady, faithful beat as I rested my head on his chest. It reminded me of God's steadiness and faithfulness throughout my life.

I thought of how God comforted my fear of being left alone at summer camp. How Jesus' strong arms saved my life when the bus pressed in on me. How he fed me in Mexico and gave me a sober father on the most special day of my life. And now, he had given me a husband to provide the heart-healing physical touch I so longed for. Mark may have wrapped me in my chrysalis of cotton and manly arms, but I knew Jesus was using my husband to do it on his behalf.

"God's not going anywhere, and I'm not, either," my new husband affirmed.

"I feel safe with you," I told Mark. It felt good to trust him to never leave me. And even better to know that Jesus certainly never would!

The Heart of the Matter

The Story of Kate

Written by Karen Koczwara

It was happening again.

From the other room, I heard the sad music blast through the speakers down the hall. I raced into the kitchen and found my mother hovered over the kitchen counter, her eyes ablaze with a mixture of all-too-familiar pain and anger. In her hand, she held a razor-sharp paring knife.

"Mom, no! You don't want to do that!" I cried, lunging forward in what felt like a slow motion attempt to stop my mother from hurting herself.

But it was too late. My mother raised the knife in dramatic fashion and then sliced both her wrists in one deft move. Immediately, dark sticky blood spurted from her veins, trickling onto her palms, covering the blade and dripping onto the floor. "Leave me alone!" she cried. "Just leave me alone!"

I heard myself scream. Then I begged, "Mom! Stop, please stop!" I snatched the knife from my mother's bloody, trembling palms and tossed it onto the kitchen counter. My heart racing, I fumbled for the nearest towel and pressed her hands together to stop the bleeding. How could this be happening again?

"Aggghh," my mother cried in anguish. She tried to wrestle out of my grip, but I held on tight.

"Leave me alone, I said!" Her voice was shrill now, an octave higher than just seconds ago.

"Mom, you're hurt! You need help!" My mind raced as I tried to think quickly. I had to get her to a hospital, but I was afraid to leave her side even just for a moment. Just as panic set in, the doorbell rang. "Come in!" I cried, my voice desperate as blood soaked through the threadbare kitchen towel.

My mother's friend flew in the house and raced toward the kitchen, her face white. "Your mother called me a few minutes ago. She sounded upset." Her voice trailed off as she saw my mother's matching white face, the blood, the knife on the counter. "Oh, no! We've got to get to a hospital!"

My legs grew weak as I prodded my mother toward the door, her normally petite frame feeling twice the weight as we helped her to the car.

My own hands were now covered with blood, a horror scene just a few feet behind us. I thought she'd been doing better now that I was in high school, and now this! When would it ever end?

"She'll be okay," my mother's friend promised as she hopped behind the wheel. But her eyes were wary, fearful, for we'd both seen this before.

"I hope so," I whispered.

Oh, please, let her be okay! Please!

The Heart of the Matter

In children's storybooks, farms are happy places, complete with cheery red barns, beautiful horses, sprawling houses and green pastures. The family wakes when the rooster crows and comes together over home-cooked dinners around the kitchen table when the sun goes down. Farms are where life begins, a place where childhood dreams are birthed, a center where all things grow. But sometimes, those storybook farms aren't fairytales after all. Sometimes, it's there that pain first lays its roots. And sometimes, it's where fear first rears its ugly head.

I grew up on a farm in Southern California. My father was a rancher, following in the footsteps of his father, raising Black Angus cattle and sheep and planting large fields of soft white cotton and fragrant alfalfa hay. Chickens, turkeys and Border Collies ran throughout our open land. I'd have preferred horses, but the dogs made fine friends, too. An outdoor playhouse served as the perfect getaway on a hot summer afternoon; sometimes, I invited the neighbor kids down the street to join in the fun. And on really good days, my father took me for rides on his tractor, hoisting me on his lap as we slowly rolled down the dirt road, a hint of dust misting our clothes. Sometimes my brother, nine years my senior, and my sister, who was five years older, would ride in the back of the planter, pouring in the seed for the next crop.

When I was nearly 4, my mother gave birth to a little boy. I wasn't too sure about having a new brother. I liked being Daddy's girl. When my father lifted him onto his lap on the tractor and rumbled down the road, I watched sadly from the porch, wondering if he'd forget all about me now that he had another son. But when he would sing his little song about my blue eyes and how he loved me and plant a big kiss on my cheek, I smiled to myself, knowing I'd always be his girl. But our relationship with Dad was not the same for all of us. My older brother often was subjected to angry, unfair treatment by my dad. Later, we would learn that my dad had been singled out by his own father for abuse.

One summer, when I was 7 years old, my parents sent me to stay with my grandparents for a few weeks. "Now, remember, you listen to Grandma and Grandpa, and do whatever they say while we're gone," my mother reminded me, planting a kiss on my head.

"Okay," I replied obediently. "I will."

On a muggy afternoon, my grandfather called me into the garage. He sat on a stool, the baseball game blaring on the radio as he waved me forward with a smile. "Hi, sweetie. Come sit by Grandpa for a minute."

I walked toward him and climbed into his lap. "You like baseball?" he asked, nodding toward the radio.

I shook my head. "Not really," I mumbled.

"I didn't think so," he said, laughing. He leaned down and kissed my cheek, his stubble scratchy against my smooth skin. And then, to my horror, he molested me. "There, there, Grandpa is just loving you," he whispered into my ear.

I froze, my blood growing cold. Something about this

felt very, very wrong, but I didn't dare say a word. Afterward, I wriggled out of his grip and tried not to look into his eyes.

"Now, this is our little secret, okay?" he said softly. "Don't tell anyone about your special time with Grandpa, okay?"

I nodded, biting my bottom lip. I wanted to run into the house and hide, but I didn't want him to think I was scared. "Yes, Grandpa," I stammered. I didn't like the garage, I didn't like baseball and I certainly didn't like what had just happened. Outside, I thought I heard footsteps on the sidewalk. What if someone had heard and knew what he'd done? What if they had seen what went on!

"Oh, there you are! I've been looking for you. Come and let's have a nice glass of iced tea," my grandmother said cheerily when I ran back into the house. "Where were you, dear?"

"Just … outside." I stared at the ground, my cheeks flaming. I felt ashamed about what Grandpa had done, but then, it wasn't my fault, was it? I hadn't done anything wrong.

"Well, go wash your hands. I've made the most delicious pound cake." My grandmother's eyes told me she had no idea that there was more than a ball game going on in that musty garage.

Later that very year, I had my first Holy Communion in the Catholic church. My mother helped me find a beautiful little white dress, complete with a dainty veil.

"Look at you, like a little bride," she whispered, smiling as she twirled me in front of the bedroom mirror. A certain sadness crept into my heart. I had read enough magazines and seen enough TV to know that brides were supposed to feel beautiful and joyous on their big day. I didn't feel beautiful anymore when I thought of my little white dress. I only felt shame. Shame that I'd let my grandfather touch me the way he had. Shame that I could not speak about it to a soul.

In the third grade, my mother decided to send my sister and me to the local Catholic school. "You will get a good education there," she insisted.

I attended a little country Catholic church with my family growing up, wriggling in my seat in my best dress as the priest walked us through a series of sayings and songs. I didn't know much about Catholic school, but I sure hoped it wouldn't be as hard to sit through as church sometimes was.

While the education at the Catholic school was indeed good, it came with a price. I sat up straight at my desk, not daring to move as my teacher, a very strict nun, traipsed around the classroom with pursed lips and stern eyes. After class one day, I realized I'd left my coat in the cloakroom. I dashed back inside to retrieve it and ran straight into her. "I … I just left my coat and need to grab it," I stammered in a small voice.

She leaned over and clucked her tongue. "You need to learn responsibility," she said airily. "Go home and write out the Ten Commandments 10 times each. Bring them back tomorrow, and only then can you have your coat."

Ten times? I could hardly remember all of the Ten Commandments, much less write them down 10 times. Obediently, I sat down, opened our family Bible and wrote out the Ten Commandments until my wrist cramped and my head hurt. It seemed like an awfully silly punishment for just forgetting a coat, but then, everyone knew better than to protest this nun.

One day, I tripped while walking to my seat. All the other kids erupted in laughter. The nun asked me to come to the front of the room and write out "I will not fall down in class" until I filled every blackboard in the room. My hand shook as I grabbed the chalk and painstakingly scrawled the words. My cheeks burned as I felt the eyes of my classmates behind me. It seemed one could get in trouble just for breathing wrong, if they were not careful. I made up my mind right then and there that I did not care for Catholic school.

I wished I could be back in the catechism class at the little country church where the nuns had been much nicer and the lay teachers had been kind. In fourth grade, my mother sent me back to public school. I was relieved to be out from under the strict nuns and back in class with my neighborhood friends. We continued to attend the little country church, and I poured myself into my schoolwork. I felt safe.

Changing Course

When I was 9, we moved to a larger home in a nearby rural community, though we kept the farm. At home, my mother's behavior grew strange. She became sad, anxious and angry for no reason. I would see her crying uncontrollably, wringing her hands and rocking back and forth in some deep sorrow I couldn't understand.

One afternoon, I came home to find my father seated in the living room, his eyes weary with concern. "Where's Mom?" I asked, dropping my schoolbooks in a chair.

My father sighed. "She's in the hospital. The doctors are trying to help her feel better."

"Because she gets so sad?" I asked slowly.

"Yes, because she gets so sad." He stared out the window, as though she might come walking up the path at any moment. "Your mother tries her best, but sometimes she just can't cope," he explained. What I didn't know was that my mom had taken pills, lots of pills, in an attempt to end her life.

When the holidays came around, we visited my grandparents again. I had come to dread these visits, when my grandfather pulled me into his garage for our "secret time." When I heard him call my name, I squeezed myself into a small space between the garage and the neighbor's fence, hoping he would not find me. But he was persistent. "There you are!" Once again, I was back in the garage.

During one such holiday visit, the house was full of

family members. A place to sleep was designated for all who were there. I was assigned to sleep with my grandfather. That night, my grandfather pushed open his bedroom door and saw me cowering on the bed. "So, you get to sleep with me tonight." He strode over and sat down beside me, pulling me in for a hug. "Has Grandpa told you he loves you today?"

I cringed, suddenly repulsed by the stench of his shaving soap and his bristly skin. I glanced up at the slightly cracked door, hoping my grandmother, or anyone for that matter, would bustle into the room and rescue me from what was about to happen. I did not want to be alone with this man. "I'm really sleepy," I mumbled to no avail. My heart raced as it often did when my grandfather came near me. I wanted to run. I wondered if all old men acted so strangely.

Before I could wriggle out of his grip, my grandfather pressed himself onto me and touched me in places I did not like. I held my breath, praying for it to be over, just as I did during the scary parts of a movie. At last, he pulled away and whispered, "Remember, Grandpa's just loving you. And this is our special little secret. You mustn't tell anyone."

I shook my head. "I won't," I promised, but I felt sick. How could I keep this little secret to myself? He nodded off to sleep, snoring loudly. I lay awake in the darkness. *Will this ever stop?* I thought to myself.

One afternoon, my cousin approached me with a strange look on her face.

"Does Grandpa ever do weird things to you?" she whispered.

My heart skipped a beat. Had my grandfather been touching my cousin, too? I stared at her, wanting to share, and for that one instance, I mustered the courage to speak up. I shook my head. "Yes," I replied, shrugging. "Why?"

"Just wondering," she mumbled, walking away. I could tell by the look in her eyes that I was not the only one who had drawn Grandpa's attention.

I wished I could talk to my mother about my grandfather's behavior, but these days, I had to tiptoe around her, not knowing what sort of mood she'd be in. She was back from the hospital, and I didn't want to make her sad again, so I decided it was probably best to keep my problems to myself. She had enough to worry about.

When I was 10 years old, my mother told us the news, "Your grandfather passed away of a stroke last night."

I was both relieved and sad. I had always loved my grandfather, but I certainly did not like what he had done to me the past few years. While I would miss the good times we'd shared, I'd never have to worry about him touching me again.

When I was 11 years old, my mom sat me down on the couch for a serious talk. "Your father and I are getting a divorce," my mother began. "We love you very much. This does not change the way we feel about you, but things are going to change around here very soon," she said.

With my older brother in college and my older sister getting married, parental custody needed to be decided for my younger brother and me. Mom explained that we would stay with her for now. When each of us turned 14, we could decide which parent we wanted to live with.

I sat frozen to the sofa, trying to breathe as I took in her words. *Divorce?* I glanced up at my mother, whose eyes were once again vacant and sad. *Why was this happening?* I wondered. *Was it because of her despondent behavior? Was it because she could flash angry? But then, so could my dad. Did it have to do with my dad's relationship with my older brother?*

Although I'm sure my parents argued, they tried not to do so in front of us kids. None of it made sense, and I really wished she would stop saying "divorce" — it was such an ugly word. I shuffled off to my room and buried myself in my homework, but for once, it was hard to concentrate on math facts. What did addition problems matter, anyway, when I had a whole set of real-life problems to deal with?

My mom was hired at the local pharmacy, and my dad moved back to the farm by himself. Not long after, my mom announced that we were moving to Burbank. "We're going to move in with Grandma for a time while I look for a job and a place for us to live."

We began our new life together. She enjoyed her new job, and I quickly made a few good friends in junior high. I threw myself into my studies as usual, signing up for advanced placement classes just to get an edge. School was my refuge, the one place I felt safe and sure of myself. I began daydreaming about college and having a career of my own someday, but I had yet to deal with the great pain that settled somewhere deep in my heart.

Soon, living with Grandma caused a big family blowup, and I was bounced around from house to house over the next couple of years. We moved into a quaint California bungalow nestled among an olive grove. Shortly after, my older brother entered the Navy to fulfill his ROTC obligation during the Vietnam War. I was now the oldest sibling living with Mom.

Mom began to drink with friends after work and came home later and later. This quickly progressed to drinking at home, followed by bouts of depression. I didn't understand much about the magic of the bottle, but I figured it must be her way of trying to drown her sorrows.

One night, I could hear her making angry phone calls — first to my aunt and then to my grandmother. Suddenly the house became very quiet, and I craned to hear from my bedroom. *Where is she? What is she doing?*

I searched room by room for her. I found her in the bathroom, wrists slit, blood everywhere, a razor blade on the floor. What 13 year old should be faced with this?

There was a knock at the door. My aunt and uncle had arrived, disturbed by Mom's phone call. They rushed her to the emergency room.

From that point on I lived with a fear of her harming herself. As I had done the night she slit her wrists, I would lay awake listening to make sure she was okay. I felt it was my mission to keep her safe, but my efforts did little to help her. Mom's cycle of drinking and depression continued, even though she managed to hold down a good job and provide for my younger brother and me.

To shorten her commute, we moved back to Burbank. I knew she continued to drink, but I didn't realize how much until I came home from school one day to find a slew of empty bottles of booze hidden away in a cupboard in the kitchen. She hadn't even bothered to throw them away. She sat slumped in a kitchen chair, her eyes vacant and sad. "Are you okay?" I asked, daring to approach her.

"Hmm?" She glanced up, but her stare went beyond me. "What do you want, Kate?"

I sighed. "Just wanted to tell you I got an A on my math test," I mumbled. I clutched my books and trudged down the hall. Once inside my room, I hopped up onto my bed and stared out the window at the neighboring houses. The dogs ran in circles, barking loudly as they played. How I wished to be so free, for life to be so simple. I wished I could fix my mother and make her sad eyes dance again, but I just didn't know how. I was supposed to be a kid, carefree and happy, yet the weight of the world had been piled on my shoulders. I loved my mother fiercely, but I was growing weary of her unstable behavior. I had no one to turn to for help.

When I turned 14, I was faced with the decision of whether to stay with my mom or live with my father. For days, I lay awake, trying to decide whom to live with. It made more sense to stay with my father, but deep down, I felt my mother needed me. With my older brother now in the Navy and my sister married and living in Northern

California, who would care for her if she continued along this path? And how unfair it would be to my younger brother, to expect him to shoulder this responsibility when it was far too heavy for me to carry. Ironically, when he turned 14, he chose to live with our dad.

One night as I drifted off to sleep, I decided to try asking God to help me make the right choice. "I know we don't talk as often as we should, but I just want to ask for your help. I need you right now," I prayed. Despite attending the Catholic church and school, I still did not understand much about God. I did believe in him, though, and I had always longed to be close to him, even when he had seemed so far away. I prayed every so often, thanking him and asking for help. I wasn't sure if he heard all my prayers, but I figured it couldn't hurt to talk to him once in a while. I decided to stay with my mom.

Like most of my peers, I dated throughout high school, went to prom and socialized on the weekends. While I kept up my grades, my resolve slowly plummeted. My mother's drinking worsened, and her erratic behavior and suicidal tendencies continued. Tired of trying to always rescue her, I left one day with a friend in the midst of one of her meltdowns. "I'm going out, Mom," I called out, slamming the door behind me. I felt awful, as I'd always tried to be there for my mother, but I couldn't be her savior forever.

When I returned home later that evening, my mother sat me down. She had a peace in her eyes I hadn't seen for some time. "After you left, I called your cousin and went with her to an AA meeting. I realized that I had to stop drinking, that it was taking control of my life. And you know what? As the leader was talking about a higher power, I realized that that higher power was Jesus. He's the only one who can help me." She began to cling to a special Bible verse, Philippians 4:13: "I can do all this through him who gives me strength."

"Mom, that's great!" I was relieved and thrilled that my mother had stepped out on her own to get help. Though my mother didn't often talk about God, I knew that she believed in him and had always tried to do the right thing, even when she was at her worst. I pulled her in for a tight hug. "You're going to be all right," I assured her through happy tears. "We both are."

From that day on, my mother never had another drink. I thought her mental problems would disappear. She was still plagued with mood swings, although she no longer wanted to end her life. There were still angry outbursts, sometimes followed by the silent treatment.

After high school, I applied to college and was accepted. The summer before I started classes, I had spinal surgery and was forced to start school in a full body cast. Determined to not let my health problems and home troubles stand in my way of success, I plunged into my courses head on. I enjoyed staying in the dorms, where I quickly made new friends.

Changing Course

"You should come with us to the Intervarsity group," my friend suggested one day after class. "I think you'd really like it. Basically, it's a bunch of Christian kids who love God and want to encourage each other on campus. It's a lot of fun."

I was determined to make college a fresh start, and joining in extracurricular activities seemed like the perfect way to do that. "Sure, I'll give it a try," I replied casually. Little did I know my life was about to change in a big way.

After attending Intervarsity for a few weeks, I realized what I'd been missing all of my life. Though I'd spent time in church, I'd never really understood that I could actually know God and experience his love. I had prayed and always believed he was there, but I had thought of him much like the nuns at the Catholic school: a looming figure, waiting for me to mess up so he could reprimand me. But as I watched these students at the group, so joyful and free, I wanted what they had. I wanted to know God for myself. I wanted to know him as a friend who would walk by my side and guide me through life when trials came my way.

Every night, a group of us in the dorms gathered for prayer. I sat through the prayers, listening in awe as they talked to God, thanking him and asking him to work in their lives. It seemed so easy, just like a conversation one might have with a loved one at the dinner table. Why had I never embraced this before?

One night, during prayer time, I bowed my head and asked Jesus to be in control of my life. "I am sorry for the wrong things I've done. Please forgive me, and be with me in every part of my life. I want to know you," I whispered.

Unsure if God had really heard me, I prayed the prayer a few more times over the next few weeks, until my friend explained that God had answered my prayer the first time. "Well, that's a relief!" I replied with a smile, thinking back to the times I'd had to write out the Ten Commandments repeatedly in school. Knowing Jesus was really a freeing thing after all!

I poured myself into college life, studying hard, making new friends and getting involved in leadership roles on campus. But most of all, I loved the new relationships I'd made with other kids who loved God. After years of loneliness, I finally had people to share my heart's desires and struggles with. And more importantly, I had God.

My aunt started attending a new church and invited my mother and me to attend. I still went home to be with my mom on the weekends and tried to care for her the best I could. Her condition was often unstable, but I could not be there every second to meet her needs. My mother was eager to attend church, though, and we both enjoyed the services. Unlike the church we'd grown up in, this place was filled with incredible joy. People sang and danced passionately as the music played, and when it came time for prayer, they did not hesitate to pour out their hearts and requests to the Lord. I loved being a part of something so real. I decided to follow the Bible's instruction to be baptized to show others that I had discovered an authentic relationship with Jesus. Ten of us from my mother's family were baptized together, including my mom.

One Sunday morning, I noticed a cute guy at church. As I glanced his way, he smiled back shyly, and I blushed. I'd never seen him before, but I was determined to get to know him. My chance came a few weeks later when we attended a camp retreat.

"Hey, you having a good time so far?" I looked up one afternoon to see the cute guy striding toward me.

"Yeah, what about you?" I patted the bench next to me, and he took a seat. We chatted for what felt like hours, until the sun set over the lake and the dinner bell rang.

"Dave," he said, extending a hand as he got up to leave. "I hope we can chat more soon."

When the camp ended, I was surprised to see him still standing out front with his bags packed. "What happened to your ride?" I asked.

He shrugged. "It left," he replied sheepishly. In reality he had sent them home hoping to get a ride with me.

My mother pulled the car around a few minutes later. "Can we give my friend a ride home?" I asked.

"Sure, hop in."

Dave and I were inseparable from then on. We talked every day, squeezing in late-night phone sessions and coffee after church activities. Dave had a heart for ministry, and I was beginning to feel led in that direction, too. We attended Bible studies together and soon fell in love. Just 10 months after giving him that ride down the mountain, we were married. I could not have found a more perfect man to spend the rest of my life with.

We bought a tiny two-bedroom house and enjoyed newlywed life together and worked with different ministries after college. Though I was just 22, we had already talked about starting a family, but we were unsure about raising kids in our crowded community. "I've heard Washington is a great place to start a family," Dave said. "Plus, there's supposed to be some really great churches up there. And I'm sure we could get more house for our money."

We prayed about moving and got counsel from our pastors at church. "God will guide you and show you if you're meant to move," they assured us.

One weekend, we drove up to Gig Harbor, Washington, a picturesque little town on the water. We'd heard of a great church there where others shared our closeness with God, and we were eager to check it out. When we pulled up at Harbor Life Church, Pastor Johnson came striding out of the building. "Hi, there! How are you?" He greeted us with a warm smile and a handshake. Even before we set foot inside, I knew we were home.

My husband and I fell in love with the beautiful community of Gig Harbor and even more in love with our new church. After moving there, we tried to start a family, but I was not able to get pregnant. I went to a fertility doctor, and he suggested I try hormones. "Maybe this is the route we're meant to go," I told my husband with a sigh. “I’m willing to give it a try.” I had always pictured several children romping around our house, and the thought of an empty nest was heartbreaking.

After trying the hormones for a few months, I noticed alarming changes in my vision. Concerned, I returned to the doctor. “I’m not sure I should keep taking these if they’re affecting my eyesight,” I told him.

“Well, there’s the route of artificial insemination. That would be the next step,” he explained.

I talked it over with Dave, and we prayed, asking God what he wanted us to do. We didn’t feel comfortable with the artificial insemination process, so we decided to stop pursuing fertility treatments. It was a devastating decision, but in the meantime, we began to think about adoption. “There are so many kids out there who need homes. Maybe we are meant to be a mom or dad to one of them,” I told Dave, trying to stay optimistic.

A friend called one day with some news. “My daughter is pregnant. She’s been using crack and is probably going to be giving her baby up for adoption. We’d really love for you to consider adopting the baby.”

At first, my heart soared. Perhaps this was God’s answer for our lives! Dave and I continued to pray and grow excited about the possibility of adopting the child, but as reality set in, we began to re-think things. The baby would most likely be born with special needs. Would we be the best parents for the child, or would someone else be more fit to raise the baby with all the challenges it might endure?

Our friend called again one day with an update. "Our daughter has decided to go another direction. I'm so sorry," she said quietly.

"It's okay. God is working it all out for the best," I assured her. As I hung up the phone, I prayed, telling the Lord how heartbroken I was, but also thanking him for intervening in the situation. I was learning to trust in his ways, even when they did not make the most sense to me.

"Kate, ministry is where God has you," my pastor told me one day. "I clearly see your gifts and know that he has called you to many good things."

Though Dave and I still grieved the children we would never have, we also grew excited about what God had in store for us. I started finding ways to help and encourage the women around me. It was as simple as holding events where friends could gather, listen to each other and, most important, try to listen to God together by reading the Bible.

Dave started doing the same thing with men, and we even got to do some of this work with international organizations. God had given me a heart for women, and I got involved with the women's ministry. Dave organized small groups of people to meet for encouragement and prayer, like I had experienced at my college group. He also helped men. Our ministry expanded both inside and outside our church as we joined forces with larger organizations like the Voice of the Martyrs, Aglow International and World Vision. Though Mother's Day and Father's Day still dealt painful blows, I carried the promises of God in my heart, reminding myself that only he knew what was best for my life.

One day, a Christian psychologist came to our church to speak on sexual abuse. I attended his seminar, and as he spoke, a chill shot up my spine. "I want you to take a look at the board here," he began. He wrote out several symptoms, including trust issues, extreme mood swings, depression and alcoholism. "If many of these symptoms represent you or someone you love, there is a strong chance that sexual abuse has occurred."

I sucked in my breath as he continued to share about the many signs of sexual abuse. These symptoms mirrored my mother's symptoms to a T. Was it possible she had been sexually abused as a child? After the seminar, I approached the psychologist's associate. "I just wanted to share my story with you," I began. My heart raced as I told her what my grandfather had done to me and how my mother's behavior had worsened over the years. "I thought that my grandfather had just became a dirty old man," I explained.

"No, that's not the case," she replied. "Your grandfather's behavior most likely began long, long ago with your mother. This would explain her erratic, intense behavior."

I was both devastated and relieved to learn this news. At last, I had answers for my mother's mental illness. But this also meant she'd chosen to repress her abuse her whole life. Would I be able to help her break free?

I called my mother, took a deep breath and shared

with her not only what I'd learned at the seminar, but what my grandfather had done to me. She sobbed uncontrollably for a long time before speaking. "Yes, yes, I think he could have done the same thing to me. I had to sleep with my dad for a number of years."

"I'm so sorry, Mom. I think you should get help," I told her. "There are lots of great counselors who can help you sort through your pain."

My mother sought counseling shortly after and called me in tears. "It all came back. Everything. I can't believe it," she cried. "And when it was happening, he would just keep repeating, 'I'm just loving you,' over and over," she explained through her tears. "I was just a little girl." Her voice drifted off into a heart-wrenching wail. I had not told her what he would say to me, and now she was telling me the very same words he had used with her.

"It's okay, Mom. We're going to be okay," I assured her through my own tears. With God's help, I had forgiven my grandfather long before, but I still had my own road of healing to walk down. For years, I relived the memories of that garage in my mind. I struggled with paranoia whenever I thought someone could see or hear me doing something. I stuffed my own pain, choosing instead to focus on school, my career and social things. God had brought me so far in my journey, showing me how to love my husband, how to serve him and how to be a friend to others, but the pain of my childhood always haunted me. I was grateful for answers and relieved to know why my mother had behaved the way she did all those years, but bitterness had crept into my heart without me ever realizing it.

Mom was free from alcohol and had medication to help the depression, yet I struggled to forgive her. Though her outbursts were less frequent now, they triggered a rush of emotion in me as they sliced open old wounds.

One day, I went to my family doctor for my routine mammogram. He came back with the results and a puzzled look on his face. "There's a density issue," he began. "It's probably nothing, but we'd better do an ultrasound just the same."

My sister had fought breast cancer, and I knew this increased my odds of having the disease. I agreed to the ultrasound, expecting a routine procedure with routine favorable results. But the technician's face told me something was wrong. "We need to do a biopsy right now," she said soberly. Twenty minutes later, I was having a needle biopsy done.

The biopsy revealed devastating news. I was in stage three of a very aggressive form of breast cancer. "It has most likely been developing for six years, but we missed it because of the density issue," my doctor explained. "We need to start you on treatment right away."

I drove away that day, my head in a fog, my heart racing as I processed the news. *Cancer*, the ugly C-word. I had certainly had my health struggles over the years, but I had never imagined cancer would be on my plate, too. When I told Dave, I said, "I've heard of God healing people miraculously. I think he is willing and able to do the same for me. After all, he gets all the credit when miracles happen."

Dave pulled me into his arms. "But sometimes, Kate, there isn't a miraculous healing. Sometimes God gets praised for helping you through the experience," he said gently. "I've been praying about this, and I believe God is saying there are things he wants to teach you that you can't learn any other way."

I wasn't sure I liked his view very much. I believed God was bigger than this. He could heal me this very minute, if he desired. But what if Dave was right? What if God chose to take me down a long road instead? Could good really come of that, too?

After undergoing genetic testing, I had a lumpectomy, 13 lymph nodes removed, chemotherapy, radiation and a regimen of oral medications. The treatment left me weak and severely fatigued, and though I tried to carry on with my ministry duties, I often had to retreat home for naps. I grew angry with God, wondering why he chose for me to endure such painful treatment instead of healing me on the spot. Hadn't I been through enough in life? Was this distraction really necessary for my spiritual growth?

One day, fatigued emotionally, physically and spiritually, I shared my frustrations with a friend. "I'm just so disappointed. Why didn't God just give me a miraculous healing?" I cried.

"You know, Kate, the Bible speaks a lot about bitterness and forgiveness. You shared about your mother and your struggle to forgive her all these years. Is it possible you've allowed that bitterness to fester all this time?"

This wasn't the answer I'd expected, but deep in my heart, I knew he might be right. I went home that night and thought long and hard about what he'd said. I opened my Bible and turned to the many passages on forgiveness. One, in particular, stood out. Ephesians 4:32: "Be kind and compassionate to one another, forgiving each other just as in Christ God forgave you." I had truly never forgiven my mother, never really addressed the pain she'd caused me and chosen to let it go. Although I would start out speaking well of my mom, I realized how often I would spiral into rehashing the painful past and complaining about current struggles I had with her. Though I had shared with other women about the great power of God's healing love, I never fully gave this issue to God myself. Suddenly, I knew just what I needed to do. I needed to turn my hurt over to God, once and for all, and I needed to forgive my mother from the depths of my heart.

"Lord," I prayed, "I am so very sorry. I have allowed this bitterness to fester for years, never fully forgiving my mother for the pain her mental issues caused our family. Please forgive me, and help me to forgive her. Help me to love her and see her just as you do, a broken person who tried her best to love me. Thank you for cleansing me of this." When I opened my eyes, I felt more free than I had in years, as though I had literally been washed clean and given a beautiful fresh start. What joy came from choosing to forgive, what relief when turning my pain over to Jesus and letting him carry it rather than trying to carry it myself.

As I went through the healing process in my cancer treatments, I continued to research the horrible disease and made some remarkable discoveries. Cancer, I learned, is an immune system disease, and the white blood cells in our bones are where our immune system begins. As I read my Bible, I discovered verses that seemed to describe this. One in particular stood out. Proverbs 3:7-8: "… fear the Lord and shun evil. This will bring health to your body and nourishment to your bones." How fascinating that long before cancer had a name, God spoke such things in the Bible. It was interesting to learn that choosing to hold on to bitterness could truly affect not just my spiritual health, but my physical health as well.

When I was declared cancer free, I rejoiced, but I had something even more important to sing about: I was bitterness free! I was free to love my mother just as she was. And God was about to put that love to the test once more.

Two years after my cancer diagnosis, my mother was diagnosed with Alzheimer's. Dave and I prayed and felt that it would be best to move her to a safer place. She was struggling to get by in her little apartment on her own and would now require round-the-clock care. We moved her into an assisted living home, and I agreed to be her primary caretaker. While it would mean a lifestyle change for all of us, I was truly happy to care for my ailing mother in her older age. Our time left together was precious, and I did not want to waste one more minute not showing her all the love I could give.

Caring for my mother while regaining my own health was not always easy, and sometimes she could be difficult. But I clung to those same words from Philippians 4:13 in the Bible that had helped my mother. "I can do this through him who gives me strength." My mother was a gift from God, and I drew from God's strength when my mother and I grew weak. After my mother's diagnosis, my father passed away. He had continued to live on the family farm with my younger brother until his last days. A freak accident had left him brain damaged, and his mind had never been the same since. But on his deathbed, my sister showed him a card with a picture of Jesus on it.

"Who's that?" she asked him.

"That's my Lord," he replied assuredly.

Though my father had struggled with his own story of abuse growing up, which had led to an abusive relationship with my older brother, I truly believed he had grown close to God in his last days, and I took great comfort in that. Our family may have been broken, but we would all be united together in a perfect home in heaven someday.

The Heart of the Matter

"Mom, here's your laundry, all folded and ready to go," I said as I helped her back to her chair. Her frail arm gripped mine as we slowly walked across the room. "Can I talk to you for a minute?" I asked.

"Sure, sure." She sat down in her recliner, weary from the short trip across the room, and took a deep breath. As I gazed into her eyes, now crinkled around the edges, I no longer saw an emotionally disturbed woman but a mother who had truly done her best to work hard and love her children. I put my arm around her and began. "Mom, I want you to know that for many years I harbored bitterness toward you and the things you did, but I have completely forgiven you. God has been so good to forgive me, and I want to go forward just loving you and serving you while you're here."

My mother smiled. Her withered fingers entwined with mine, and we sat there, quiet, just two girls together. In that moment, all was forgotten. We were back on the farm of my childhood, carefree as the wind, all our troubles and hurts behind us. We had each other. We had today. And today was what mattered.

Conclusion

My heart is full. When I became a pastor, my desire was to change the world. I wanted to see the people around me encouraged and the hurting filled with hope. As I read this book, I saw that passion being fulfilled. However, at Harbor Life Church, rather than being content with our past victories, we are spurred on by the belief that many more lives can be changed.

Every time we see another life change course, it increases our awareness that God really loves people, and he is actively seeking to change lives. Think about it. How did you get this book? We believe you read this book because God brought it to you to reveal his love to you. Whether you're a man or a woman, a logger or a waitress, blue collar or no collar, a parent or a student, God is passionate about reaching you. He is passionate about reaching us. He is passionate about pulling all of us from the hellish pain that's weighed us down. He offers real joy and real life that will last forever through faith in Jesus Christ.

Do you have honest questions that such radical change is possible? It seems too good to be true, doesn't it? Each of us at Harbor Life Church warmly invites you to come and check out our church family. Freely ask questions, examine us and see if we're "for real." Then, if you choose, journey with us at whatever pace you are comfortable. You will find that we are far from perfect. Our scars and, sometimes, open wounds are still healing, but we just want you to know God is still completing the process of authentic life change in us. We still make mistakes in our journey, like everyone will. Therefore, we acknowledge our continued need for each other's forgiveness and support. We need the love of God just as much as we did the day before we believed in him.

If you are unable to be with us, yet you intuitively sense you would really like to experience such a life change, here are some basic thoughts to consider. If you choose, at the end of this conclusion, you can pray the suggested prayer. If your prayer genuinely comes from your heart, you will experience the beginning stages of authentic life change, similar to those you have read about.

How does this change occur?

Recognize that what you're doing isn't working. Accept the fact that Jesus desires to forgive you for your bad decisions and selfish motives. Realize that without this forgiveness, you will continue a life separated from God and his amazing love. In the Bible, Romans 6:23 reads, "For the wages of sin [seeking our way rather than God's way] is death, but the free gift of God is eternal life through Christ Jesus our Lord" (NLT).

Believe in your heart that God passionately loves you and wants to give you a new heart. Ezekiel 11:19 reads, "I will give them singleness of heart and put a new spirit within them. I will take away their stony, stubborn heart and give them a tender, responsive heart" (NLT).

Believe in your heart that "if you confess with your mouth that Jesus is Lord and believe in your heart that God raised him from the dead, you will be saved" (Romans 10:9 NLT).

Believe in your heart that because Jesus paid for your failure and wrong motives, and because you asked him to forgive you, he has filled your new heart with his life in such a way that he transforms you from the inside out. Second Corinthians 5:17 tells us that "… anyone who belongs to Christ has become a new person. The old life is gone; a new life has begun" (NLT).

Why not pray now?

"Lord Jesus, if I've learned one thing in my journey, it's that you are God and I am not. My choices have not resulted in the happiness I hoped they would bring. Not only have I experienced pain, I've also caused it. I know I am separated from you, but I want that to change. I am sorry for the choices I've made that have hurt myself and others and denied you. I believe your death paid for my sins, and you are now alive to change me from the inside out. Would you please do that now? I ask you to come and live in me so that I can sense you are here with me. Thank

you for hearing and changing me. Now please help me know when you are talking to me, so I can cooperate with your efforts to change me. Amen."

Gig Harbor's unfolding story of God's love is still being written — and your name is in it.

I hope to see you this Sunday!

Tyson Lash
Harbor Life Church
Gig Harbor, Washington

We would love for you to join us!

We meet Sunday mornings at10:30 a.m. at
4417 56th Street NW, Gig Harbor, WA 98335.

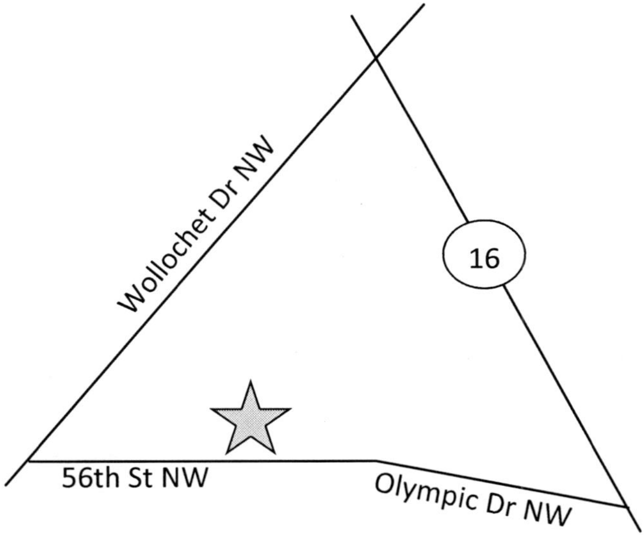

Please call us at 253.851.1734 for directions, or
contact us at www.theharborlife.com.

For more information on reaching your city with stories from your church, please contact Good Catch Publishing at www.goodcatchpublishing.com

GOOD CATCH PUBLISHING

Did one of these stories touch you?
Did one of these real people move you to tears?
Tell us (and them) about it on our reader blog at
www.goodcatchpublishing.blogspot.com.